D1757214

WITHDRAWN
FROM
UNIVERSITY OF PLYMOUTH
LIBRARY SERVICES

SEVEN DAY LOAN

This book is to be returned on
or before the date stamped below

17. DEC. 1998 CANCELLED

10. MAR. 1999 CANCELLED

2 3 NOV 2000

2 4 APR 2001

- 2 MAY 2001

- 9 MAY 20...

2 5 SEP 2001

UNIVERSITY OF PLYMOUTH

PLYMOUTH LIBRARY

Tel: (01752) 232323
This book is subject to recall if required by another reader
Books may be renewed by phone
CHARGES WILL BE MADE FOR OVERDUE BOOKS

NEGOTIATING WITH THE CHINESE

This book is dedicated to
Chamkaur, my husband
and
our daughter, Mindy

Negotiating With The Chinese

GOH Bee Chen
LLB (Hons)(Malaya); LLM (Cambridge); SJD (Bond)
Advocate & Solicitor of the High Court of Malaya

Dartmouth

Aldershot • Brookfield USA • Singapore • Sydney

© Goh Bee Chen 1996

All rights reserved. No part of this publication may be reproduced, stored in a retrieval system, or transmitted in any form or by any means, electronic, mechanical, photocopying, recording, or otherwise without the prior permission of Dartmouth Publishing Company Limited.

Published by
Dartmouth Publishing Company Limited
Gower House
Croft Road
Aldershot
Hants GU11 3HR
England

Dartmouth Publishing Company
Old Post Road
Brookfield
Vermont 05036
USA

UNIVERSITY OF PLYMOUTH

Item No. 900 341795 2

Date -3 NOV 1997 S

Class No. 302.30951 GOH

Contl. No. 1855218895

LIBRARY SERVICES

British Library Cataloguing in Publication Data
Goh, Bee Chen
  Negotiating with the Chinese
  1.Negotiation - Cross-cultural studies 2.National
  characteristics, Chinese
  I.Title
  302.3'089951

Library of Congress Cataloging-in-Publication Data
Goh, Bee Chen.
  Negotiating with the Chinese / Goh Bee Chen.
    p.   cm.
  Includes bibliographical references and index.
  ISBN 1-85521-889-5
  1. Negotiation. 2. Negotiation–Cross-cultural studies.
  3. Chinese–Psychology. I. Title.
  BF637.N4G63 1996
  302.3'0951–dc20   96-30777
                                                    CIP

ISBN 1 85521 889 5

Printed in Great Britain by Antony Rowe Ltd, Chippenham, Wiltshire

Contents

Preface   *vi*

1   Introduction: Negotiating In The Pacific Century   1

2   Cross-Cultural Perspectives On Sino-Western
        Negotiation   15

3   The Homocentric Chinese   47

4   The Psychology Of Chinese Negotiation   85

5   The Art Of War At The Round Table   133

6   Case Studies In Sino-Western Negotiation   165

Bibliography   *187*

Index   *195*

Preface

Negotiation constitutes an integral part of the lawyering process. Cross-cultural negotiation, particularly in the Sino-Western context, is especially topical as a consequence of the economic shift to the Asia-Pacific region. This book aims at offering insights into Chinese-style negotiation which is vastly different from Western ways based on the governance of respective cultural norms. The Chinese are collectivists who subscribe to the values of mutual dependence and conformity. As a result, their negotiating approach tends to be relational. In contrast, Westerners are individualists who cherish independence and individual creativity, and who are therefore inclined towards a transactional negotiating style. The Chinese, in addition, are a strategy-minded people. Various military strategies originating from ancient warfare have been passed down by means of folklore and proverbs to instil in the Chinese a strategic approach in the conduct of daily lives. This is made possible by the fact that the Chinese do not have a divisive view of knowledge and generally regard all knowledge as inter-related. Negotiating with the Chinese need not be exasperating or frustrating; one only has to be familiar with the Chinese mental software. Bearing in mind that the Chinese are both relational and strategic, understanding them can prove to be a fascinating and rewarding experience.

I am indebted to many people for their help and goodwill. I have talked to numerous people and obtained their insights on Chinese negotiation and it is impossible to thank them all, but I wish to extend my sincere thanks to the respondents whose names appear in Chapter 6. I record my gratitude and appreciation to Bond and Harvard Universities for excellent research facilities and collegial assistance. I owe a constant debt to my parents and siblings for their love and guidance, and I register an undying debt to my late beloved grandparents.

Finally, two persons in this world deserve the credit for bringing this book to fruition: Chamkaur, my husband, for his abiding support and patience, and Mindy, our baby daughter, for creating an environment of immeasurable joy and inspiration.

GOH Bee Chen
May 1996   Bond Law School, Australia

1 Introduction: Negotiating In The Pacific Century

Introduction

The hard truth about negotiation is that it is basically a psychological game. What you want out of it depends on what you expect from the other person's ability and willingness to accommodate. In a monocultural setting, one's psychological menu may be drawn from one's education, training, experiences and environmental conditioning which may, in turn, aid one in some speculative accuracy or predictability in handling others. The challenges, however, become manifold when one's negotiating context shifts to the cross-cultural environment. Such an environment is, in today's terms, inevitable. Global facilitation of transport and communication in our Information Age necessitates increased frequency of cross-cultural contact and linkages. The need for cross-cultural knowledge in the field of inter-personal communication is not only essential, but urgent. According to Hall, 'when cultures meet, because the steps are different few people know where they are'.[1] Negotiating with the Chinese represents a fresh challenge to most skilled negotiators who are consciously unaware of the interplay of cultural norms present in Chinese-style negotiation.

It is essential to avoid a tendency to stereo-type or to generalize.[2] To cite Hendon and Hendon: 'Trouble arises when we refuse to abandon the stereotypes in favour of the unique reality of the actual persons we are dealing with'.[3] The solution may lie in realizing that the conduct of human affairs leads to certain patterns of behaviour, which, over time, produce certain congruous and consistent results.[4] To quote Hsu, 'in spite

1

of exceptional individuals and regional differences, a majority of the people of each society do act according to their society's accepted and usual patterns of behaviour in their day-to-day business of life'.[5] As a consequence, it is possible to formulate certain basic recurring themes and generalizations.[6] All cross-cultural negotiators must, however, bear in mind the uniqueness of each negotiation despite their firm grasp of cross-cultural behaviour and learn to exercise flexibility in varying contexts.[7]

My initial research on comparative - Chinese and Western - socio-legal approaches occurred about fourteen years ago when I undertook a jurisprudential study on the Chinese attitude towards dispute resolution. Since then, I have systematically noted the respective cultural differences towards questions pertaining to law, justice and politics, and towards life in general. My own personal experiences, and numerous personal accounts from others, as well as organised research findings have consistently supported a coherent observation regarding Chinese and Western behaviour patterns. References to 'the Chinese', 'Western' and 'the Westerner(s)' as used in this book must, however, be qualified here.

The term 'the Chinese' is not a reference to the nationally identified group of people found in China. Rather, it is an ethnic reference and encompasses the Chinese resident in China as well as, for instance, in Hong Kong, Taiwan, Singapore and Malaysia.[8] As Lague puts it, 'Despite generations away from the mainland, intermarriage and sometimes the loss of their ancestral language, the overseas Chinese have clung tenaciously to their Chineseness.'[9] Similarly, Kao observes, 'What we think of as Chinese now encompasses an array of political and economic systems that are bound together by a shared tradition, not geography'.[10] Research has found and supported the notion that the Chinese people tend to consider themselves culturally Chinese and are unmindful of the political conception.[11] 'Chinese people tend to behave in the same manner whether they are in China, Taiwan or Hong Kong.'[12] In Bo Yang's observation, 'No matter what country a Chinese may be living in, he will always remain Chinese first and other Chinese will continue to see him as

Chinese'.[13] In this regard, Chinese-style negotiation may be seen to be applicable to a Chinese-Malaysian or Chinese-Australian provided, as it were, that this Chinese person by and large still exhibits Chinese cultural traits.[14] An education in Mandarin in a Chinese person's formative years is a good indicator of his or her inclination towards traditionalist Chinese ways. However, it would be wrong to assume or conclude that *all* Chinese are the same. Such is not my intention. My reference to the Chinese in its ethnic sense, rather than the political sense, must needs be moulded by the sociological background and cultural conditioning of such Chinese peoples. The narrow sense of the term 'the Chinese' as used in this book, therefore, applies to the ethnic Chinese who subscribe, to a large extent, to traditional Chinese ways, values and norms.

The terms 'Western' and 'Westerner' are used to describe primarily persons of Anglo-Saxon ethnic origins. For example, Western literature on 'Negotiation' has been in the main authored by Americans; and as Hall puts it, 'while the United States has absorbed millions of people from countries around the globe, *the core culture of the United States has its roots in northern Europe or Anglo-Saxon culture*'.[15]

It will be demonstrated that the Chinese and the Westerners practise divergent negotiating styles. The Chinese style of negotiation is characteristically relational. In contrast, the Western approach to negotiation is basically transactional. With regard to the Chinese, Koller's following observation regarding the Chinese encapsulates the general Chinese attitude which in turn influences Chinese-style negotiation: '[For the Chinese] The human world is primary; the world of things is of secondary importance'.[16] In a similar vein, Smith observes that 'the Chinese world is a human world dominated by social relationships'.[17]

Negotiation As A Lawyering Skill

Negotiation is an integral aspect of communication and deals with process, not substance.[18] It is a function of the communicative behaviour of humankind. We negotiate all the time with the people around us. Ironically, most often, negotiation represents an unconscious activity to us despite our constant involvement with it. In the context of the legal profession, negotiation is an important lawyering skill. As legal professionals, it is important that we develop effective negotiation skills. We can then be of better service to our clients. The average person tends to associate lawyers with law, and forgets that lawyers deal with law in association with people. Lawyers advise and represent clients on a variety of matters, ranging from business or commercial negotiation, family matters to litigious issues. Lawyers, therefore, negotiate all the time whether in professional or personal capacities.[19] As negotiation is very much concerned with process, our polished skills will enhance our ability to articulate our substantive knowledge. A skilled negotiator is one who is able to reach an agreement with the other side in a win-win situation.

About a decade ago, Professor Roger Fisher of the Harvard Law School pointed out that 'all lawyers negotiate, but few of us have either a conceptual understanding of the process or particular skill in it. It is time to recognize negotiation as a field for specialization'.[20] Of late, law schools have begun to pay particular attention to teaching 'Negotiation' as a specialized lawyering skill.[21] Like every skill, it is impossible to impart all knowledge. A skill has to be learnt, developed and consistently practised in order for one to achieve a certain competency level. Also, much depends on the learner's aptitude, personality, willingness to learn and continuing or persisting experience and polishing.[22] However, directed and intensified learning may help: 'study, theory and concentrated experience can make a big difference. Lawyers can learn to produce wiser outcomes, and to do so more efficiently and amicably'.[23]

In this Information Age, where global communication is the norm and speed its essence, it is imperative that humanity develop means of understanding cross-cultural behaviour and establishing effective and meaningful communication.[24] In order to be a competent negotiator, the negotiator has to realize that each negotiating experience is different from the next.[25] The experience one has accumulated from past negotiation may enlighten one as regards particular aspects of human nature but it certainly is no guarantee of an exact application in the next negotiation.[26] This is because a fundamental aspect of every negotiation is that it involves the intricacies of inter-personal dynamics.[27] As Zimmerman points out, 'Interpersonal skills are critical.'[28] In the cross-cultural sense, even if one has a good grasp of the other party's cultural traits, it is equally important to take note of the personal traits and predisposition of one's negotiating counterpart.[29] This is due to the fact that one's negotiating counterpart may not always exhibit his or her cultural tendencies.[30]

In cross-cultural negotiation, people in general are governed by their respective cultural norms, and most of the time unconsciously. As Hall remarks, 'culture controls behaviour in deep and persisting ways, many of which are outside of awareness and therefore beyond conscious control of the individual'.[31] Unless we pay attention to the ever-present cultural nuances, we may be misled into thinking that people behave in the same way and should negotiate no differently.[32] Cross-cultural behaviour can appear baffling and confusing to the untrained, since it is human tendency to judge the other person through one's accustomed habits,[33] and one is hardly able to avoid projecting one's 'ethnocentric yardsticks and assumptions'.[34] Misunderstandings can easily arise due to the fact that we tend to base and interpret another's actions by our own instinctive frame of reference.[35] As Lakoff contends,

> We assume the possibility of direct transfer of meaning, that a gesture or act in Culture A can be understood in the same way by members of Culture B. Often this is true:

there are universals of behaviour, but as often that is a dangerous assumption; and by cavalierly ignoring the need for translation, we are making misunderstanding inevitable.[36]

To Culture A, what may seem incomprehensible behaviour in Culture B is often a result of ignorance.[37] And prejudice is often a product of such ignorance. It is often necessary to get closer to a different culture in order to understand it. By attempting to achieve such understanding, one may be surprised to find that there are underlying common traits prevailing in different cultures. As Hsu vividly puts it:

Like the spider's web, a people's behaviour, infinitely complex though it may appear from a distance, has a common thread and a clear design.[38]

Our task in improving human relations is to attempt to discover this 'thread' and trace the 'design'. If we are able to understand and obtain an insight into another way of life quite alien to our own, we can seek to enhance communicative interaction.[39]

Engaging in a Sino-Western negotiation can be a challenging exercise due to the underlying divergent values held respectively by the Chinese and the Westerners. Such cross-cultural negotiation extends beyond an understanding of basic human psychology. It calls into question one's usual perceptions, insights and prejudices.[40] One is constantly invited to re-assess one's basic assumptions.[41] To echo Carroll: 'one of the great advantages of cultural analysis, aside from that of expanding our horizons, is that of transforming our cultural misunderstandings from a source of occasionally deep wounds into a fascinating and inexhaustible exploration of the other'.[42]

In another instance of cross-cultural negotiation involving the Japanese and the Westerners, an American attorney, Robert Walters, advises as follows :

An attorney's failure to appreciate or become familiar with the importance of the cultural influences which affect the Japanese client or party often reveals itself at a critical stage of the transaction, and the results can be disastrous.[43]

The above advice may similarly be applied in respect of Sino-Western negotiation. For instance, the Japanese and the Chinese alike are generally not predisposed to written contracts.[44] Their attitude is that mutual trust between the parties is more important than written contracts.[45] A lawyer engaged in such cross-cultural negotiation may be sensitive to this factor and be able to render professional advice accordingly.[46]

Culture-bearers tend to carry their own meanings and perceptions of words, often resulting in a divergence rather than a convergence of thought in cross-cultural communication. Learning cross-cultural behaviour in a negotiation is necessary and enlightening, and a challenging experience. As Bedi puts it, 'Cultural understanding is difficult and sometimes painful to attain, but the rewards can be also high'.[47] But, one should not try to stereotype cross-cultural behaviour to the point of endeavouring to become or imitate the other person.[48] Effective Sino-Western interaction does not imply that the Chinese become Westerners, or the Westerners, Chinese: 'Be a good Western businessperson rather than a bad imitation of an Asian businessperson.'[49] The results otherwise may prove to be counter-productive.[50] The successful international or cross-cultural negotiator should, therefore, be a negotiator who has a keen sense of awareness of cultural differences.[51]

The Pacific Century

The Mediterranean is the sea of the past, the Atlantic is the ocean of the present, and the Pacific is the ocean of the future.[52]

Weiss writes: 'The shape of the next century is being cast in the Pacific'.[53] The dawn of a new century heralds the era of the Pacific, and could perhaps bring to fruition the prophecy of John Hall cited above. As we move closer to the Twenty-First Century, appropriately styled the 'pacific century',[54] we realize more and more that the world's economic focus is shifting to the Asia-Pacific region.[55] Technological advancements have resulted in globalization at a much rapid pace. In particular, innovations in information technology have brought the world community even closer.[56] There is now a greater facility in the movement of people and things across the oceans. Such mobility has resulted in increased cross-cultural contact.[57] It is no longer sufficient for one to think nationally and locally. The modern world requires one to think and act globally.[58] Cross-cultural knowledge is a pre-requisite to an enlightened existence. In the context of corporations, Bedi remarks thus: 'Only those organisations which are able to become multicultural will survive and prosper in the pacific century'.[59]

The case now and for the future is one with increased Sino-Western interaction, especially as the Western world pays greater heed to Asia's economic growth.[60] In the Asian region, one is faced with a substantial portion of the players being of Chinese origin. The Chinese presence can hardly be ignored. Kao describes this presence as the 'Chinese Commonwealth'.[61] As he observes, 'Chinese businesses -- many of which are located outside the People's Republic itself -- make up the world's fourth economic power'.[62]

For example, in Australia, the most recent statistics revealed that in 1991-1992, China's investment in Australia stood at $1.407 billion, with further rise anticipated.[63] Additionally, 'the greater part of Australia's trade is now with Asia, and economic realities are obliging Australians to adjust their social attitudes.'[64] The latest (1991) Australian statistics also showed that there were 227,400 ethnic Chinese resident here.[65] In this regard, it is relevant to note that 'persons of Chinese ethnicity constitute over one-quarter of the world's population.'[66] A recent press report entitled 'Great Wave of China' indicates the following Chinese census:

> Hong Kong and Taiwan account for about 26 million of the overseas population, followed by Indonesia with 7.2 million, Thailand with 5.8 million, Malaysia with 5.3 million, Singapore with 2.1 million, Burma with 1.5 million, The Philippines with 1.2 million and Vietnam with 0.8 million.

> There are also about 1.8 million ethnic Chinese living in the rest of Asia and Australasia, 1.8 million in the United States, 1 million in Latin America, 0.6 million in Canada, 0.6 million in Europe and 0.1 million in Africa.[67]

With China adopting an open door policy, the economic presence of the Chinese will be more greatly felt than it already is with the strong economies of Hong Kong, Taiwan and Singapore.[68] To cite Chan and Chen, 'with the increase in business activities between China and western countries, the urge to learn more about China goes beyond a sense of common curiosity. Western businessmen often complain about the difficulties in negotiating business with China, without knowing that the Chinese are masterful in the arts of negotiation and planning'.[69] In a similar vein, Chu states as follows:

> Since the re-opening of China in the late 1970's, the Chinese have been criticised in the West for unconventional business and political behaviour. But the strategies that underlie the behaviour of the mainland Chinese are not very different from those of the people of Japan, Korea, Taiwan, Hong Kong, or Singapore. Because international business has a longer history in those countries, the people there have had an opportunity to adapt their negotiating techniques for use in dealing with the Western world. Their techniques are not really different from the original concepts and strategies the Chinese use, but are simply an updated version.[70]

In accordance with global trends, Sino-Western interaction is definitely on the increase.[71] It is, therefore, of fundamental importance to develop a deep, rather than a superficial, understanding of Sino-Western communication.[72] A superficial knowledge is insufficient to advance real understanding. The Westerner needs to transcend from his or her ability to use chopsticks at meals, to cultivating his or her knowledge of the Chinese habits of thought.

NOTES

1   Edward T. Hall, *Beyond Culture,* Anchor Books/Doubleday, New York, 1976, 1981, at page 156.

2   Donald Hendon and Rebecca Angeles Hendon, *World-class negotiating: Dealmaking in the global marketplace,* John Wiley & Sons, Inc., New York et al, 1990, at pages 50-51; William Gudykunst, *Bridging Differences: Effective Intergroup Communication,* Sage Publications, Newbury Park (California), 1991, at pages 71-78.

3   Donald Hendon and Rebecca Angeles Hendon, note 2 above, at page 51.

4   Francis L.K. Hsu, *Americans and Chinese: Passage to Differences,* The University of Press of Hawaii, Honolulu, 1953, 1981 (third edition), at page 2; Chin-ning Chu, *The Asian Mind Game: Unlocking the Hidden Agenda of the Asian Business Culture - A Westerner's Survival Manual,* Rawson Associates, New York, 1991, at page 7.

5   Francis L.K. Hsu, note 4 above, at page 2.

6   Michael Bond and Kwang- Kuo Hwang, "The Social Psychology of the Chinese People" in Michael Harris Bond (ed.), *The Psychology of the Chinese People,* Oxford University Press, Hong Kong/Oxford/New York, 1986, at pages 227-229; Christopher Smith, *China: People and Places in the Land of One Billion,* Westview Press, Boulder/San Francisco/Oxford, 1991, at pages 39-40; Chin-ning Chu, note 4 above, at page 7.

7   William Gudykunst, note 2 above, at pages 104-105 and 122-125.

8   Lynn Pan, *Sons of the Yellow Emperor: The Story of the Overseas Chinese*, Mandarin Paperbacks, London, 1990, Reprint 1991, at pages 375-377; This notion of being a Chinese was echoed in a Symposium on 'Cultural Identity and Social Integration of the Chinese in Australia' held on the Gold Coast on 1 June 1994, an event attended by around a hundred participants and the Chinese originating from China, Taiwan, Hong Kong, Singapore, Malaysia and Australia.

9   David Lague, 'Great Wave of China' in The Weekend Australian, 12-13 March 1994.

10   John Kao, "The Worldwide Web of Chinese Business" in (1993) 71 *Harvard Business Review*, at page 24.

11   Michael Harris Bond and Kwang-Kuo Hwang, note 6 above, at pages 226-229; Christopher Smith, note 6 above, at page 39.

12   S. Tamer Cavusgil and Pervez N. Ghauri, *Doing Business in Developing Countries: Entry and Negotiation Strategies*, Routledge, London and New York, 1990, at page 123.

13   Bo Yang, *The Ugly Chinese*, quoted in Chin-ning Chu, note 4 above, at page 205.

14   Chin-ning Chu, note 4 above, at page 149.

15   Edward T. Hall and Mildred Reed Hall, *Understanding Cultural Differences*, Intercultural Press, In., Yarmouth (Maine), 1990, at page 140 (original emphasis by the authors); see also Edward T. Hall and Mildred Reed Hall (1987), *Hidden Differences: Doing Business with the Japanese*, Anchor Press/Doubleday, Garden City, New York, 1987, at page xix.

16   John M. Koller, *Oriental Philosophies*, Charles Scribner's Sons, New York, 1985 (second edition), at pages 246-247.

17   Christopher Smith, note 6 above, at page 41.

18   As pointed out by Professor Emeritus Roger Fisher, formerly Williston Professor of Law at Harvard Law School, at a meeting in his office in Harvard Law School on 18 June 1993 whilst I was a Visiting Researcher at Harvard Law School during the summer of 1993.

19   Roger Fisher, "What About Negotiation As A Specialty ?" (1983) 69 *American Bar Association Journal* 1221, at page 1222.

20   Roger Fisher, note 19 above, at page 1221.

21   The Harvard Negotiation Project is world renowned. At the Bond University School of Law, the Dispute Resolution Centre has

gained recognition throughout Australia in the teaching of lawyering skills such as negotiation, mediation and arbitration.

22   Roger Fisher, note 19 above, at page 1223.

23   Roger Fisher, note 19 above, at page 1223.

24   Donald W. Hendon and Rebecca Angeles Hendon, note 2 above, at pages 11-12.

25   William Gudykunst, note 2 above, at pages 20-22; S. Tamer Cavusgil and Pervez N. Ghauri, note 12 above, at pages 88-89 and 129.

26   Pierre Casse and Surinder Deol, *Managing Intercultural Negotiations*, Sietar International, Washington, D.C., 1985, at page 133.

27   Robert M. March, *The Japanese Negotiator: Subtlety and Strategy Beyond Western Logic*, Kodansha International, Tokyo and New York, 1988, at pages 10-11.

28   Mark A. Zimmerman, *Dealing with the Japanese*, Unwin Paperbacks, London & Sydney, 1985, at page 129.

29   Mark A. Zimmerman, note 28 above, at pages 128-129.

30   Robert M. March, note 27 above, at page 11.

31   Edward T. Hall, *The Silent Language*, Greenwood Press, Publishers, Westport (Connecticut), 1959, at page 25.

32   Edward T. Hall and Mildred Reed Hall (1987), note 15 above, at pages 3-4.

33   William Gudykunst, note 2 above, at page 3; S. Tamer Cavusgil and Pervez N. Ghauri, note 12 above, at page 129.

34   Francis L.K. Hsu, note 4 above, at page xxii.

35   William Gudykunst, note 2 above, at page 13; S. Tamer Cavusgil and Pervez N. Ghauri, note 12 above, at page 129; Jeffrey Z. Rubin and Frank E.A. Sander, "Culture, Negotiation and the Eye of the Beholder" (1991) *Negotiation Journal* 249, at pages 251-252.

36   Robin Lakoff, *Talking Power: The Politics of Language*, Basic Books, New York, 1990, at pages 165-166, quoted in William Gudykunst, note 2 above, at page 13.

37   Edward T. Hall (1959), note 31 above, at page 25.

38   Francis L.K. Hsu, note 4 above, at pages 11-12.

39   William Gudykunst, note 2 above, at page 5.

40   William Gudykunst, note 2 above, at pages 61-71.

41   William Gudykunst, note 2 above, at pages 2-7; Pierre Casse and
     Surinder Deol, note 26 above, at pages 80-83; see also Robert
     Moran and William Stripp, *Dynamics of Successful International
     Business Negotiations*, Gulf Publishing Company, Houston, 1991;
     Frank Acuff, *How to Negotiate Anything with Anyone
     Anywhere Around the World*, American Management
     Association, New York, 1993.

42   Raymonde Carroll, *Cultural Misunderstandings*, quoted in Hari
     Bedi, *Understanding the Asian Manager: Working With the
     Movers of the Pacific Century*, Allen & Unwin, Sydney, 1991, at
     page 2.

43   Robert J. Walters, "'Now That I Ate the Sushi, Do We Have a
     Deal ?' - The Lawyer As Negotiator In Japanese-U.S. Business
     Transactions" (1991) 12 *Northwestern Journal of International
     Law & Business* , at page 335.

44   Robert J. Walters, note 43 above, at pages 345-346, 356 and 359;
     Mark A. Zimmerman, note 28 above, at pages 91-104; Chin-ning
     Chu, note 4 above, at pages 239-240; Edward T. Hall, *The Dance
     of Life: The Other Dimension of Time*, Anchor Press/Doubleday,
     New York et al, 1983, at page 104; Edward T. Hall and Mildred
     Reed Hall (1987), note 15 above, at pages 128-129.

45   Mark A. Zimmerman, note 28 above, at pages 91-92; Jerome Alan
     Cohen, *Contract Laws of the People's Republic of China*,
     Longman, Hong Kong, 1988, at page 23.

46   Robert J. Walters, note 43 above, at pages 346-347 and 356-359.

47   Hari Bedi, note 42 above, at page 2.

48   Lucian Pye, *Chinese Negotiating Style: Commercial Approaches
     and Cultural Principles*, Quorum Books, New York et al, 1992, at
     page 110.

49   Chin-ning Chu, note 4 above, at page 245.

50   Chin-ning Chu, note 4 above, at pages 260-261.

51   Edward T. Hall (1983), note 44 above, at page 103; S. Tamer
     Cavusgil and Pervez N. Ghauri, note 12 above, at page 87.

52   Uttered more than a hundred years ago by the American
     statesman, John Hay. Quoted in Hari Bedi, note 42 above, at page
     35.

53   Julian Weiss, *The Asian Century: The Economic Ascent of the
     Pacific Rim - and What it Means for the West*, Facts on File, New
     York/Oxford, 1989, at page vi.

54   Hari Bedi, note 42 above, at pages 59, 162 and 171.

55   Julian Weiss, note 53 above, at page 8; Robert Elegant, *Pacific Destiny: Inside Asia Today*, Hamish Hamilton, London, 1990, at page 12.

56   Donald Hendon and Rebecca Angeles Hendon, note 2 above, at page 12; Robert E. Allinson, 'An Overview of the Chinese Mind' in Robert E. Allinson (ed.), *Understanding the Chinese Mind*, Oxford University Press, Hong Kong/Oxford/New York, 1989, at page 23.

57   Donald Hendon and Rebecca Angeles Hendon, note 2 above, at page 49.

58   Hari Bedi, note 42 above, at page 171.

59   Hari Bedi, note 42 above, at page 171.

60   Robert Elegant, note 55 above, at page 12.

61   John Kao, note 10 above, at page 24.

62   John Kao, note 10 above, at page 24. The other three being North America, Europe and Japan.

63   Appeared in Sue Williams' interview with Henry Tsang, Sydney's Deputy Lord Mayor, The Weekend Australian, 12-13 March 1994.

64   Lynn Pan, note 8 above, at page 362.

65   The Weekend Australian, 12-13 March 1994.

66   Michael Harris Bond and Kwang-Kuo Hwang, note 6 above, at page 227.

67   Review article by David Lague, The Weekend Australian, 12-13 March 1994.

68   Michael Harris Bond and Kwang-Kuo Hwang, note 6 above, at pages 228-229; Christopher Smith, note 6 above, at page 40; John Kao, note 10 above, at page 24.

69   M.W. Luke Chan and CHEN Bingfu, *Sunzi on the Art of War and its General Application to Business*, Fudan University Press, Shanghai, 1989, at pages 5-6.

70   Chin-ning Chu, note 4 above, at page 11.

71   Lucian Pye, note 48 above, at page viii.

72   S. Tamer Cavusgil and Pervez N. Ghauri, note 12 above, at page 126.

2 Cross-Cultural Perspectives On Sino-Western Negotiation*

Introduction

Human communication is often thought of as something physical, scientific, and tangible.[1] But, increasingly, this perception is being questioned.[2] If a human being is conceived of in both physical and spiritual terms, then, it is also necessary to analyse the spiritual (or non-tangible) part of human existence: human consciousness.[3] Essentially, communication is a 'multichannelled and multidimensional process for handling meanings'.[4] And meanings are not attributable to words alone. This is why nowadays attention is being paid not just to oral communication, but also to other means of human communication, for example, the emphasis placed on body language,[5] or telepathy.[6]

The subtle and unconscious use of body language as a communicator is a prevailing factor. The way one may nod in agreement, or shake one's head in disagreement has been well-noted. These gestures, though, may be interpreted differently in an inter-cultural context, according to the meanings attributed to such gestures in particular cultures, and awareness or otherwise of what they mean could spell the success or failure of a negotiation.[7]

In many ways, it is important to realize that when human beings negotiate, their desire is to achieve mutually beneficial gains. But, most of the time, this is not easy because each side often cannot second-guess what the other side really wants. This is where misunderstandings may occur, and both negotiating parties could suffer from bruised feelings, frustration, irritation and annoyance. Not everyone will be able to understand perfectly at any given instant what the other party wants. Negotiation therefore is a process whereby both parties attempt to achieve respective wants through discourse and interaction.[8]

Negotiation is concerned with the art of communication. When two parties of different cultural backgrounds try to communicate, the sum total of their communication techniques is not made up of words alone.[9] More truly, they find themselves being subject to a host of unconscious forces in the form of behavioural patterns, attitudes and prejudices.[10] These forces are the underlying elements of culture passed down, learned and cultivated over the generations.[11] Because most of the time cultural forces are the unconscious part of our behaviour, we tend to find ourselves not being aware of culture and the role it plays in a negotiation.[12] Such ignorance on our parts may be the factor why there could be a communication breakdown.[13] This is due to the fact that when there is cross-cultural interaction, the respective parties tend to be unaware of the 'manifold unstated, unformulated differences in their structuring of time, space, materials, and relationships',[14] with the result that these very differences often lead to a 'distortion of meaning, regardless of good intentions'.[15] In a cross-cultural context, it is not surprising why communication becomes a more formidable and challenging task.[16]

With regard to Chinese and Western cultures, each has been the product of enduring civilizations, and each culture has shown the varying approaches in the governance of human affairs -- be they political, economic or social.[17] Yet, very often, we do not apply ourselves consciously in a cross-cultural (Sino-Western) context. As Hall remarks, 'Culture hides much more than it reveals, and strangely enough what it hides, it hides most effectively from its own participants.'[18] In a similar vein, Barnlund observes thus: 'What each person otherwise does is to act naturally, that is, according to the dictates of his or her own cultural premises, and how does one explain acts that are so natural that they spring from sources of which the actors themselves may be unaware ?'[19] Such lack of awareness can especially be linked to the Western view of 'the cultural unconscious'.[20] As a matter of fact, it is only recently that the Western world has started paying attention to such a concept.[21] As for the Chinese, they are generally attuned to the presence of cultural factors in communication. Nevertheless, the respective societies have focussed on their own cultural traits and such 'cultural projection always has been a stumbling block on the path to better understanding'.[22]

Usually, we tend to judge others by our own value yardsticks.[23] We tend to evaluate the behaviour of another party by the way we ourselves might respond in a similar situation.[24] However, given the opportunity for self-reflection, we realize how futile, and dangerous, such an evaluation can be.[25] 'The assumption that everywhere men and women inhabit the same world and assign essentially the same meanings to events of their lives is perhaps the most pervasive and most intractable barrier to intercultural rapport'.[26] This is because we tend to allow our prejudices to guide us, instead of discarding these prejudices and being open-minded to cultural differences.[27] Given the context of one culture or another, we may find that we need to make adjustments, suspend our habits, and accommodate differences.[28] We may discover, too, that our prejudices are unfounded; that other people are accustomed to a particular system of behaviour, like us, and that in such diversity we should increase our awareness, understanding and sensitivity rather than maintain our personal biases against the ways of others dissimilar to our own.[29]

The Role Of Culture

What is culture ? The definition is not an easy one. Dodd terms it 'the total accumulation of many beliefs, customs, activities, institutions and communication patterns of an identifiable group of people'.[30] Gudykunst refers to it as   the 'system of knowledge'.[31] Culture provides us with our 'internal models of reality'.[32] I would define culture as the habits of our ways. These habits have been learned and cultivated over time and almost become second nature to us. Culture seems to be the backdrop against which we operate, to a large extent in an unconscious way.[33] It represents and encapsulates the way of life of a particular group of people.[34] Behaviour patterns and attitudes which have been built up over the years affecting a group of people may come to constitute some form of cultural code for its actors. The cultural code seems nebulous, yet operative.[35]

As human beings, we are in fact conditioned beings.[36] Our actions are based on our knowledge, memory, predispositions and our learning.[37] Our conditioning is further enhanced by our group environment. We behave in a particular way which is expected of us by our peers and our contemporaries.[38] We become accustomed to certain habits because they have been socially approved, either expressly or tacitly, in the environment in which we operate or find ourselves in: in short, 'many dynamisms are a function of habit'.[39]

Whenever there appears a need for us to deviate from our pattern of behaviour, or to traverse in another cultural environment, our instinctive action is to base our actions on our customary behaviour, and, quite naturally, to expect the other party to behave in a manner not unlike our own.[40] In short, the average person tends to engage in ethnocentric behaviour.[41] If that other party does not, questions immediately spring to our mind of that party's deviation.[42] Confusion arises. Often, the knowledge that that other party has a different culture and, therefore, has different ways, may not occur to us as we continue to judge and evaluate and mould the other party in our own image.[43]

Our unconscious interpretations of another person's behaviour may tend to yield unexpected outcomes. As an example, Professor Roger Fisher[44] described to me an experience he encountered in Pakistan. While trying to make an appointment with a high official, he enquired from the latter as

to what time would suit him. The official told him, 'Any time.'
A time was subsequently fixed for 10 am the next day. Professor
Fisher's local guide warned him that the Pakistani official was
only trying to be polite, and did not in actual fact mean it. He did
not believe the local guide. However, it turned out to be true, and
it turned out to be a frustrating experience for Professor Fisher.

The above example can be subsumed under Beck's five
principles of cognitive therapy which illustrate how
misunderstandings may occur:

(1)   We can never know the state of mind - the
attitudes, thoughts and feelings - of other people.
(2)   We depend on signals, which are frequently
ambiguous, to inform us about the attitudes and wishes of
other people.
(3)   We use our own coding system, which may be
defective, to decipher these signals.
(4)   Depending on our own state of mind at a particular
time, we may be biased in our method of interpreting
other people's behaviour, that is, how we decode.
(5)   The degree to which we believe that we are correct
in divining another person's motives and attitudes is not
related to the actual accuracy of our belief.[45]

It is human tendency not to grant concessions regarding
the other person's uncustomary behaviour.[46] It is human
tendency to doubt, to question, rather than to understand and to
accommodate.[47] In such instinctively excluding systems we often
find that we enlarge the gaps of differences, and often make no
attempt at bridging them.[48] Polarized communication seems to
be encouraged.[49] What otherwise can be made to be understood
becomes suddenly an impossible task. We pursue our aims
relentlessly, while ignoring the opportunity for human
enlightenment. We concentrate on making deals, while forgoing
the opportunity to establish mutual cross-cultural
understanding.

Culture And Language

Casse and Deol warn that even though 'language is an important link across cultures and between people ... it is also a barrier'.[50] This is because words convey different meanings to different people, in accordance with their perception of reality.[51] We tend to base our respective perceptions of reality upon our own frame of reference. Various meanings, therefore, become possible from the same single event, depending on our dimension of seeing.[52] For example, I experienced the following during a recent cross-cultural interaction.[53] In a gathering comprising predominantly Australians of Western origin, I announced that my favourite colour was blue. The colour blue conveys to me a sense of space and eternity. My Australian counterparts immediately concluded that my reference to space was territorial, and that, therefore, I would enjoy privacy, exclusivity, and non-interference from others. I quickly pointed out that the reverse was more true, i.e., my meaning of space is all-inclusive and universalistic. In this case, one could see that words and their meaning became different. The difference is attributable to our respective frames of reference: the individualistic or egocentric Australian relates space to privacy, giving primacy to the self, whereas my collectivistic or homocentric Chinese background relates space to the universe, giving primacy to the community.

Though it is helpful for one to learn the language of another, this does not necessarily result in mastering another culture.[54] In fact, Hall calls it 'the paradox of culture'[55] that 'language, the system most frequently used to describe culture, is by its nature poorly adapted to this difficult task'.[56] This is because language does not act as an instrument of transferring reality, but rather, as a means by which information is received and processed by the brain.[57] In other words, language may translate words, but not meaning. In cross-cultural negotiation, one expects that knowledge of the language of the other party is an asset, and facilitates negotiation. However, language alone is not sufficient. Without also knowing the other party's culture, one is in danger of not extracting a particular meaning intended in a negotiation.[58] Culture embraces language, and, in the process of negotiation, knowledge of both is paramount. Yet, it is a common misperception by a negotiator that knowledge of another's language is mastery over the other party's culture. Knowledge of another person's language provides one with glimpses into the other party's cultural behaviour. However, such cultural empathy does not necessarily equal cultural understanding. The way towards understanding another's culture is through experience.[59]

It is natural to expect that people from different cultures speak different languages. But, as Hall points out, what is more important to realize is that they 'inhabit different sensory worlds'.[60] 'It is not simply that people speak in different tongues but also that they see differently, think differently, feel differently about their experience'.[61] Experience is a facet of culture. The ability to speak a foreign language is not enough. To understand culture, one has to delve into the psyche of another, and attempt to learn the way of life of the other person. In short, to become the other.[62]

The following is an illustration of the contrasting attitudes of two different cultures -- the Americans and the Japanese -- towards language:

> In the United States language is respected as a way of clarifying positions, of comparing and contrasting views, and a way, ultimately, of testing the relative merits of divergent opinions. Words are the primary tool of disclosure. In Japan words are somewhat distrusted and seen as less reliable guides to a complex and elusive reality; words are *a*, but not *the*, means of communication. The nonverbal channels, though less precise, seem better suited to the expression of feelings, and feelings may be more significant than facts.[63]

Harumi Befu makes the following accurate and incisive remark: 'One crucial thing about learning to be Japanese is to know what people mean without (their) saying it.'[64] At this juncture, it is important to realize that whilst the American may view language as an instrument for clarity and for logical analysis, their Japanese counterpart is more at ease with ambiguity, and views language 'as a means of promoting harmony'.[65]

In fact, the above characteristics of the Japanese could apply equally well to the Chinese, since both peoples share a similar cultural tradition.[66] For example, a Chinese father whose values are deeply embedded in tradition, may feel slighted as a consequence of a particular incident involving his adult child. In all probability, he will remain stoically silent, expecting the child to know the cause of his displeasure without his uttering it.

Sino-Western Cultures

In order to understand the respective Chinese and Western cultures, it may be useful to begin by observing the family and socialization process of an individual.[67] The following scenarios attempt to show how the two cultures may differ in their outlook and perceptions. The fundamental differences may help to shed some light on inter-cultural communication, particularly with regard to the respective ways and styles of negotiation between the Chinese and the Westerners.

My background is Chinese-Malaysian. I grew up in a small village in Malaysia with a predominantly Chinese population.[68] Here, as in many similar villages, it is common for a stranger to ask a child: 'What is your father's name ?' It is through one's family that one's place in society is established.[69] Chinese society is essentially based on a system of kinship, in which the self occupies a place within this web of relationships.[70] In the above illustration, being asked about one's father goes to show that one's identity is based on, and traced through, one's kin. A child becomes significant because of his or her family, not because of who he or she is.[71] Such a culture has its genesis in a homocentric conception, more popularly characterized as collectivism.

One might wish to contrast the above position with the example of an Australian child of Anglo-Saxon origin (an example of a Western child).[72] When you come across this child, it is rather natural to ask merely: 'What is your name ?' The child's place in society is a matter of right, independent of the family.[73] It can be seen that Western society is fundamentally based on an egocentric conception, better known as individualism. The individual self is of primary importance. It has an existence independent of its immediate social structure - the family.[74] The child is trained from young to make his or her own decisions, and to be responsible for his or her own choices.[75] The tendency is towards individual self-actualization.[76]

Triandis remarks that it is the relative emphasis[77] on collectivism and individualism by the diverse cultures that may determine social behaviour.[78] He goes on to say thus:

> In individualist cultures most people's social behaviour is largely determined by personal goals that overlap only slightly with the goals of collectives, such as the family, the work group, the tribe, political allies, coreligionists, fellow countrymen, and the state. When a conflict arises between personal and group goals, it is considered acceptable for the individual to place personal goals ahead of collective goals. By contrast, in collectivist cultures social behaviour is determined largely by goals shared with some collective, and if there is a conflict between personal and group goals, it is considered socially desirable to place collective goals ahead of personal goals.[79]

It can, therefore, be observed that within an individualistic culture, initiative is admired whereas within a collectivistic culture, conformance is expected.[80] Such a value departure bears an impact upon a person's perception of reality. As Gudykunst states: 'People in individualistic cultures tend to be universalistic and apply the same value standards to all. People in collectivistic cultures, in contrast, tend to be particularistic and, therefore, apply different value standards for members of their ingroups and outgroups.'[81]

In the case of collectivists, communication behaviour depends on whether or not one is a member of an ingroup or of an outgroup.[82] This is due to the fact that 'self-definition is based on the groups one belongs to'.[83] In such a society, 'an ingroup is a group whose norms, goals, and values shape the behaviour of its members'.[84] An example is one's family. An outgroup 'is a group with attributes dissimilar to those of the ingroup, whose goals are unrelated or inconsistent with with those of the ingroup, or a group that opposes the realization of ingroup goals (competing)'.[85] Such a definition of an outgroup suggests the possibility of conflict. However, in relation to Chinese collectivism, the underpinning philosophy is one of eventual harmony between ingroups and outgroups in social behaviour. Such grouping is perceptual, and changes in accordance with one's association.[86] This type of group distinction appears to be irrelevant to people who are individualistic,[87] since individualism emphasizes the self and not the group.

The collectivism-individualism dichotomy is central to the understanding of cultural variability in a cross-cultural negotiation.[88]

Collectivism : The Chinese Example

I do not intend to suggest that all members of a particular culture behave in a homogenous fashion, nor is it my intention here to offer stereotypes or over-simplifications concerning particular peoples. What, however, may be observed is that there are certain fundamental traits that may consistently appear so as to form a coherent and systematic pattern of behaviour which, in turn, makes it plausible for certain generalizations to occur.[89] Cultural behaviour affecting a group may offer some model of behaviour; but, to think that every member of such a group necessarily falls into such a description would be erroneous. After all, human behaviour is a result of a package of conditioning, training and influences.[90] As such, though it is useful to be able to recognise some regular and consistent traits, it by no means should be assumed that the definitions are invariable. What is important to realize, though, is the fact that human beings are part of the natural order of things and are therefore capable of self-organising tendencies. By this is meant that every group of people may tend towards a particular type of behaviour, which, in the context here, may be referable to collectivism or individualism, but such a tendency is not absolute. Such a tendency at best enables that group of people to exhibit a dominant style tending towards, say individualism, but it does not mean that this group is precluded from exhibiting collectivistic traits. In every situation, the demonstration of a particular tendency is one of degree. What may be generalized is that on average, the Chinese tend to be collectivistic or homocentric, and the Westerners tend to be individualistic or egocentric. In the words of Gudykunst,

> Individualism and collectivism both exist in every culture, but one tends to predominate. Cultures in which individualism tends to predominate include, but are not limited to: Australia, Great Britain, Belgium, Canada, Denmark, France, Germany, Ireland, Italy, New Zealand, Sweden, and the United States. Cultures in which collectivism tends to predominate include, but are not limited to: Argentina, Brazil, China, Costa Rica, Egypt, Ethiopia, Greece, Guatemala, India, Japan, Kenya, Korea, Mexico, Nigeria, Panama, Saudi Arabia, and Venuzuela. Generally, most Arab, African, Asian, and Latin cultures are collectivistic.[91]

Collectivism emphasizes the social unit - be it family, society, community or country - as the central functionary.[92] The individual is merely a part of, and is subservient to, the larger whole. The actions and reactions of an individual are tied to the immediate social unit.[93] The individual is not encouraged to act or feel publicly as an individual, but to do so out of a sense of socially-obligated conformity.[94] As Hsu observes, the problem for the Chinese 'has always been how to make the individual live according to accepted customs and rules of conduct, not how to enable him to rise above them.'[95] The Chinese way of life is, by and large, one such example of collectivism.[96] 'The Chinese child learns to see the world in terms of a network of relationships. He not only has to submit to his parents, but he also has little choice in his wider social relationships and what he individually would like to do about them.'[97] The Chinese are, therefore, accustomed to a collectivist pattern of behaviour.

The traditional Chinese way of life has been much shaped by Confucian precepts.[98] Confucianism stresses the five cardinal relationships : that between emperor and subject, father and son, husband and wife, elder brother and younger brother, and friend and friend.[99] These relationships are viewed in a hierarchical order.[100] Each actor assumes the role in relation to the other. The observance of one's place within this set of hierarchical order gives rise to the attainment of social harmony. In a collectivist system, the aim of human association is the preservation of social harmony.[101] Collectivists internalize the norm of being of service to others, "without doing any sort of utilitarian calculation. It is not a case of 'What's in this for me ?'"[102] As a consequence, what is valued is collaborative action.[103] This necessarily precludes the individual's self-assertions, for one's assertiveness would run counter to social harmony.[104] The dictates of social harmony place value on compromises, and a preoccupation with the interests, not the rights of the members within a particular social unit. As Edward de Bono observes in relation to the Japanese who are also collectivistic, 'Japan has produced many highly creative people but on the whole the Japanese culture is oriented towards group behaviour rather than individual eccentricity. Traditional Japanese culture has not put a high value on individual creativity (in contrast to the West)'.[105]

The preoccupation with social harmony necessarily suggests that the establishment of relationships or friendships is important. Occasions for it can often be found in the partaking of meals. The Fourteenth Dalai Lama of Tibet, when in China as a guest in 1954, observed thus: 'These banquets were considered to be very important by our hosts, who seemed to be of the opinion that genuine friendships could develop just by people sitting together at the dining-table.'[106]

A collectivistic or homocentric society emphasizes inter-dependence. Within the Chinese context, one may trace it to the Confucian emphasis on inter-relatedness.[107] Each one is regarded as a part of the larger system. Great expectations are placed on mutual dependence in daily lives. Individualism is shunned and scorned. Hsu further observes that this trait of mutual dependence is 'so deeply embedded and so satisfying socially and psychologically'[108] to the Chinese that one is prepared to give up one's material wants in order to be around one's immediate social relations.

In summary, collectivism values 'reciprocity (*pao*), obligation, duty, security, tradition, dependence, harmony, obedience to authority, equilibrium, and proper action (*li*)'.[109] It is interesting to note that these values import a great deal of societal dimension, and further emphasize the relational aspect of the Chinese culture.

Individualism : The Western Example

Individualism, or egocentrism, is imbibed with self-centredness.[110] The concept of individualism emphasizes the self above all else.[111] It is the individual person, not the community in which the individual belongs, that has significance and meaning. Therefore, unlike collectivism, an egocentric person's reference point is not one's group, but one's own self. Heavy emphasis is placed on self-realization.[112] A person is allowed and encouraged to create, and attain, self-expression in a theoretically free society.[113] The individual is the focal point of all activities. As Waterman states:

> Each person is viewed as having a unique set of talents and potentials. The translation of these potentials into actuality is considered the highest purpose to which one can devote one's life. The striving for self-realization is

accompanied by a subjective sense of rightness and personal well-being.[114]

Individualism gives rise to self-expression, self-creativity, and self-preservation.[115] In Emerson's words, 'whoso would be a man, must be a non-conformist.'[116] That which is greatly cherished is one's independence.[117] There is great pride in being individualistic in society, and society is but a larger reflection of self.[118] Assertiveness is paramount, for, without it, the individual cannot survive in an egocentric environment.[119] This is because the guiding norm for an egocentric society is competition.[120] For instance, competition pervades every sphere of American life:

> The struggle of children for the attention and affection of parents, the struggle of parents to win their children's approval, the concern of American women for beauty and style, the anxiety of the husband to prove he is successful and thus deserve his wife's affection, the competition for success in all organizations, the readiness of the churches to vie with each other for membership are traced to aspects of United States individualism.[121]

The egocentricism in Western society contrasts the individual with the group. 'The fundamental assumption of modernity, the thread that has run through Western Civilization since the 16th Century, is that social unit of society is not the group, the guild, the tribe, the city, but the person.'[122] The individuals who form part of this society come together as disparate selves, not as a harmonious unit like the Chinese example. The individual learns early in life that to get ahead, one must take charge of one's own life and destiny.[123] The individual tends to do things to please himself or herself, to do what is enjoyable and not be dictated by some other authority.[124] The concept of mutual dependence, prevalent in a collectivistic society, is alien to the egocentric being.[125] Rather, the egocentric person is accustomed to being self-reliant, independent and individualistic.[126]

The goal of an individual in an egocentric environment is to find true self-creativity in the enhancement of material welfare.[127] Hence, it is important for such an individual to fight for rights in pursuit of justice, not to focus on mutual interests.[128] The purpose of human association is to increase one's material comfort in a utilitarian fashion. When asked to do something, an individualistic person's common response is: 'What's in this for me?'[129] Social happiness is measured in material, quantifiable, terms.[130]

In individualism, the emphasis on independence and self-reliance tends to deter the forming of lasting relationships evident in the collectivist cultures.[131] The idea of independence is in order to not rely on other people. It may be said that in the pursuit of materialism, which is the ideal of individualism, the egocentric person is often confronted with a sense of human isolation, loneliness and alienation.[132]

Given the contrasting cultures, the communicative processes of the collectivistic person will tend to differ from the individualistic person. The conception of collectivism-individualism provides a useful framework in explaining the other major dimension of cultural variability, high-context and low-context communication.[133]

High-Context And Low-Context Communication

Cross-cultural communication can be both an intriguing and taxing exercise, due to its propensity to incur misunderstandings. We noted earlier that the facility of language is no assurance of complete cultural insight. All too often, we have seen how words may be misunderstood, gestures misinterpreted, and meanings mishandled. As Han points out:

> Each culture has its own particular climate which the culture-bearers engender as they proceed in the art of conversation, which is the highest of all arts, and the most

perilous, since it is exchange of thought and feeling through the dangerous manipulation of words. When two culture-bearers confront each other, then what is said by one is heard quite differently by the other ...[134]

It is therefore essential, when engaging in a cross-cultural discourse, to be mindful of the underlying cultural factors and nuances lest they distort reality.[135]

We live in an Information Age. The information we receive depends on how we process it and interpret it in order to arrive at meaning. Meaning, in turn, depends very much on the context in which the information is given.[136] The process of contexting becomes an important function for communication to be effective.[137] In this connection, one has to realize, too, that how one does the contexting is referable to whether one is more accustomed to a high-context culture or to a low-context culture.[138] In the former situation, the emphasis on communication is indirectness and ambiguity.[139] In the latter situation, communication is predictably direct, and explicit.[140]

High-context and low-context communication is largely a reflection of social and organizational behaviour, with the result that a collectivistic society is more preoccupied with high-context communication and an individualistic society is more attuned to low-context communication.[141] This owes to the fact that collectivists are 'sensitive to situational features and explanations, and tend to attribute others' behaviour to the context, situation, or other factors external to the individual'.[142] In contrast, individualists are 'sensitive to dispositional characteristics and tend to attribute others' behaviour to characteristics internal to the individual (e.g. personality)'.[143]

Hall states: 'A high-context communication or message is one in which most of the information is either in the physical context or internalized in the person, while very little is in the coded, explicit, transmitted part of the message'.[144] 'Internalized' here means that external norms seem to be assimilated by the collectivist so that much is left unsaid and the listener is then expected to extract the message from what has been said. The

Chinese who are collectivists are, therefore, more used to high-context communication.[145] This is because in a collectivistic society, one views inter-personal relationships as extremely important and there is, therefore, a tendency 'to pay attention not only to what is said, but also to the context of what is said - the gestures, the orientation of the body, the objects associated with what is being said.'[146] In consequence, the Chinese tend to communicate in an indirect, ambiguous and roundabout way.[147] Hall makes the following perceptive observation regarding a high-context person:

> When talking about something that they have on their minds, a high-context individual will expect his interlocutor to know what's bothering him, so that he doesn't have to be specific. The result is that he will talk around and around the point, in effect putting all the pieces in place except the crucial one. Placing it properly - this keystone - is the role of his interlocutor.[148]

On the other hand, the habit of communication of the individualistic Westerner tends to be low-context in nature, i.e. 'the mass of information is vested in the explicit code'.[149] The necessary consequence is that Westerners are inclined towards communicating in a straightforward and direct fashion.[150] Evidence may be seen in common expressions such as '"say what you mean', 'don't beat around the bush', and 'get to the point'".[151]

Without any cultural awareness, it is not surprising to discover that a Chinese and a Westerner may transact at cross purposes. Both may apply their respective internal norms and value judgements at the expense of achieving understanding. Ironically, both may think that they have arrived at an agreement only to find out later that they have each misunderstood the other. Cross-cultural negotiation is laden with each party's inherent and unconscious ways of perceiving reality and meaning. Such ways, in turn, govern their divergent approaches to a negotiation.

Sino-Western Negotiation

Negotiation is an aspect of human activity influenced by the cultural behaviour of societies. Chinese-style negotiation and Western-style negotiation may be said to be traceable to the deep-seated cultural patterns of behaviour of the respective peoples,[152] each separately and differently developed over time and exhibited as the 'historical continuity of personality and culture'.[153] These deep-seated patterns represent certain fundamental traits that have persisted and resisted the passage of time.[154] Therefore, while the conduct and behaviour of people can change over time, and new habits of behaviour may be adopted, some of the old ones are seen to be too entrenched to be forsaken. They become traditions which die hard.

In a study of cross-cultural negotiation, it is these enduring cultural traits which can be said to influence and shape the negotiation process. An understanding of such cultural traits by both parties may lead to 'cultural wisdom',[155] which means gaining an insight into respective cultures. It may enable one to begin one's new learning process of systematic thinking about culture.[156] Therefore, an understanding of the underlying cultural factors will aid the appreciation of a cross-cultural negotiation and enable one to be an enlightened negotiator.

At present, however, there seems to be an absence of such enlightenment. Given that Chinese culture is basically homocentric and high-context, and Western culture is essentially egocentric and low-context, clashes of behavioural rules come into play in a Sino-Western negotiation. Their respective thought patterns, rules of conduct, arousal and responses to feelings, originate from and advance to different points.[157] Each culture applies different value norms. For example, the Chinese pay high regard to tradition and stability, whereas the Westerner cherishes creativity and change. Organizational behaviour of the former is based on co-operation, while for the latter, it is based on competition. Such characteristics can result in the respective peoples adopting different means towards their goals. Their communicative patterns and processes highlight their respective styles.

As a consequence of the cultural differences, the Chinese tend to practise a relational approach to negotiation as contrasted with the Western transactional approach to negotiation.

A relational approach to negotiation is based on the relationship between the negotiating parties. Even though, of course, the negotiating parties are desirous of striking a deal, the finalisation of the deal is a step away from the forming of friendship between them. It is common to find, in a relational approach to negotiation, that the questions asked tend towards establishing friendships. In a Chinese negotiation, for example, the Chinese are prone to enquire after the other party's health or well-being, children's education or general welfare, or community happenings. Very often, it is only when these preliminary enquiries have been made that they come to the point of negotiating. In a negotiation, it is rare indeed to find a Chinese plunging straight to ask for something, or to begin any negotiating, without touching on any aspect of the negotiating counterpart's family welfare. 'Negotiating in the Middle East is like getting married. It involves a whole range of relationships, and hardly about the transactions themselves.'[158] Such a parallel can similarly be drawn in the context of negotiating with the Chinese in their relational approach to negotiation.

The establishment of friendship necessarily imports trust and co-operative behaviour. What is important and is emphasised in this approach is the relationship, not the transaction. The transaction is the ultimate aim: but, if the relationship-building fails, the parties are then not interested in the transaction itself.[159] A relational approach underlines the fact that negotiating parties have long-term objectives in mind, and are not dealing with each other on a one-off basis.[160] As such, their focus on relationships serves the purpose of sealing on-going transactions.[161] Considerable patience is desirable and quick gains are remote.[162]

In contrast, a transactional appproach to negotiation is one whereby the parties focus their minds and objectives on the deal itself, and try to work to achieve the finalisation of the deal. The parties involved are less concerned with the success or failure of the interpersonal relationship.[163] In fact, they view their interpersonal relationship as incidental, or perhaps, partly instrumental to the negotiation process. Friendships are viewed as being superficial, tentative and temporary.[164] There is also a lack of long term objectives.[165] Their goal is to achieve 'specific demands ... in the short term and independently of long term objectives'.[166]

For example, the American 'is inclined to be more oriented toward achieving set goals and less toward developing close human relations'.[167]

While it can be argued that in Western culture, there are relational expressions such as 'How are you?' or 'How is it going?', it is also common to find one using transactional expressions such as 'What can I do for you ?' or 'How can I help you ?' as opening statements. The latter expressions are particularly common when two parties meet or interact and one is not sure of the intention of the other party's reason for the meeting. Upon analysis, it can be seen that in Western culture, one is more interested in the doing of something, rather than the well-being of somebody. The Westerner's culture is not accustomed to enquiring after the other party's welfare. In fact, the Westerner may regard such an enquiry as an intrusion of one's privacy.

What is important is that the apparent divergence in the respective cultural approaches to negotiation must be appreciated. Otherwise, the negotiation process between the Chinese and the Westerner can be mystifying, frustrating, and non-productive. What is important is to recognise the differences, understand them, and accept them where necessary, knowing that 'behind the apparent mystery, confusion, and disorganization of life there is order'.[168]

Even though in a negotiation the Chinese are largely relational in their approach and the Westerners are chiefly transactional in their style, their communicative processes and behavioural patterns may change in accordance with their goal orientations. This means to say that, for instance, in a negotiation in which the Chinese are of the opinion that the business dealing is likely to be one-off, their negotiating strategy may come closer to the transactional model.

Similarly, there is an emerging trend on the part of the Westerners to recognise the value of relationships and how establishing relationships may enhance the negotiation process.[169]

But, it would be a mistake for one party to try to become the other party. In a cross-cultural negotiation, there may be a tendency for a party to be aware of the cross-cultural differences and then try to imitate the other party. Take the example of a Westernized and sophisticated Japanese who tried to negotiate American-style with the Americans, and the Americans on their part imitated the Japanese. Nothing worked. Each performed the other's dance steps, but there was no music.[170] Such an example points to the danger of thinking that one knows cross-cultural negotiation, resulting in blind stereo-typing and a mismatch. A communication breakdown occurs when one tries to learn about the other in a superficial way. This is no recipe for the success of the negotiation outcome. A study of cross-cultural negotiation is not about reverse role play.[171] Rather, the primary aim is to educate the parties of the cultural nuances at play and to alert them accordingly. Such an awareness will help a negotiator to be culturally prepared. In the words of Pye:

> Effective negotiating requires a constant alertness to the distinctive qualities of the Chinese to appreciate the meaning behind their actions, so as not to be misled or to mislead them. Yet, at the same time, one can only act superficially in accordance with the rules of Chinese culture. It is impossible to out-Chinese the Chinese. It is also foolish to try to, for the Chinese have had long experience in dealing with foreigners, and Chinese negotiators fully understand that foreigners are culturally different.[172]

There may be some resistance by certain quarters to the value of culture even in a cross-cultural negotiation.[173] For example, when I first met with Professor Roger Fisher[174] and discussed the subject of cross-cultural negotiation with him, he said:

> Cross-cultural negotiation is good, but it is not about teaching the other party how to negotiate in the reverse way. What is the answer then in trying to find out about cross-cultural negotiation ? There are so many cultures in the world. It is just impossible to learn them all, just as it is impossible to learn all the languages. Because it is impossible, it is also unnecessary. No doubt it is important to know and appreciate sensitivities, to know when one is not offending another due to cultural ignorance.

While I agree with Professor Fisher that one should be sensitive to other cultures in order not to offend, I seek to differ with his view that because it is impossible for one to learn all the cultures of the world, cross-cultural negotiation is not important enough to devote specific study. An interest in another person's culture enables the creation of a climate of understanding and respect. Bowman and Oda comment thus:

> People of good will can manage to reach agreements and to develop friendship in spite of difficulties encountered in the communication process. The willingness to accept differences, to suspend cultural prejudices, and to persevere in the face of misunderstandings can overcome even great differences in perceptions and expectations.[175]

The objectives of a cross-cultural study are to learn and to understand one another, to accept differences, and to try to become an effective and culturally enlightened negotiator. One must attempt to use one's judgement and wisdom in cross-cultural situations, and attempt not to stereotype or misapply one's knowledge. Human endeavours can only be better served with effective cross-cultural understanding.[176] The impossibility of learning all cultures is an insufficient reason for making the specific study of cross-cultural negotiation a peripheral task.

After all, 'the journey of a thousand miles begins with the first step'.[177]

Conclusion

An examination of cross-cultural negotiation is not only fascinating, but useful. Negotiating in a similar cultural environment is itself an unpredictable one with parties engaged in numerous tactics and strategies. Negotiating cross-culturally makes the task even more challenging. This is because it is natural human tendency to evaluate another's behaviour with reference to one's terms, and misunderstandings may, therefore, readily occur. As such, in a negotiation context in which inter-personal dynamics assume an important role, it will be fascinating to examine the adjustment, comprehension, and frustration of the different psychological paths that a cross-cultural negotiation generates.

We tend to engage in ethnocentric behaviour in a sub-conscious way.[178] When value systems are different one from the other, and when there is an automatic tendency to impose one's values on another, cross-cultural negotiation takes on a hue unknown to one used to negotiating in a predictable, familiar, and culturally similar environment. One virtually removes oneself from a safe haven to territorially unknown waters. One can then be overcome by a sense of uncertainty, hesitancy and diffidence. Under such negative conditions, one may not be able to think and function properly. Hence, the causes of untoward irritation, annoyance, misunderstanding and frustration.[179]

Understanding cross-cultural behaviour would assist one to appreciate the different ways of doing things, and to arrive at more instances of a co-incidence of thought. Its usefulness cannot be easily undermined. Society can only improve with better insights into human behaviour, feelings and thought - particularly insights into other cultures.

Gudykunst states: 'At any given point in time, our communication is influenced more by our culture than we are influencing our culture by our communication.'[180] The way the

Chinese negotiate could easily baffle anyone unfamiliar with Chinese culture. An appreciation of certain aspects of Chinese culture and their customs will greatly enhance one's understanding of the Chinese socialization process, i.e. their homocentric way of life. This is because homocentrism is significantly influential in shaping the Chinese relational approach to negotiation.

NOTES

* A substantial version of this Chapter appeared in [1994] 5 *Australian Dispute Resolution Journal* 268-284.

1 Edward T. Hall and Mildred Reed Hall, *Understanding Cultural Differences*, Intercultural Press, Inc., Yarmouth (Maine), 1990, at page 3.

2 Edward T. Hall and Mildred Reed Hall, note 1 above, at page 3.

3 See Philip Allott, *Eunomia: A New Order for a New World*, Oxford University Press, Oxford/New York, 1990.

4 Dean Barnlund, *Communicative Styles of Japanese and Americans: Images and Realities*, Wadsworth, Belmont (California), 1989, at page 190.

5 Edward T. Hall, *Beyond Culture*, Anchor Books/Doubleday, New York, 1976, 1981, at pages 71-84.

6 V. R. Burkhardt, *Chinese Creeds and Customs*, South China Morning Post Limited, Hong Kong, 1982, at page 120. In this connection, Burkhardt cites the example of the Chinese servants: 'In their relations with their servants their thoughts are often translated into action without a word being spoken, and often the wish is no sooner formed than the servant's footsteps are heard coming to execute the unuttered command.'

7 S. Tamer Cavusgil and Pervez N. Ghauri, *Doing Business in Developing Countries: Entry and Negotiation Strategies*, Routledge, London and New York, 1990, at pages 117-120.

8 Herb Cohen, *You Can Negotiate Anything*, Lyle Stuart Inc., Secaucus (New Jersey), 1980, at pages 15-16.

9 Edward T. Hall, *The Silent Language*, Greenwood Press, Westport (Connecticut), 1959, at page 99; R. Huseman, M. Galvin and D. Prescott, *Business Communication: Strategies and Skills*,

Holt, Rinehart & Winston, Sydney, 1988 (third edition), at page 225.

10 Dean Barnlund, note 4 above, at page 190.

11 Edward T. Hall (1959), note 9 above, at page 98.

12 Edward T. Hall (1959), note 9 above, at page xiii.

13 Edward T. Hall (1959), note 9 above, at page 25.

14 Edward T. Hall, *The Hidden Dimension*, Doubleday, New York, 1966, at page x.

15 Edward T. Hall (1966), note 14 above, at page x.

16 Edward T. Hall (1959), note 9 above, at pages 44 and 99.

17 See Francis L. K. Hsu, *Americans and Chinese: Passage to Differences*, The University Press of Hawaii, Honolulu, 1981, (3rd Edition).

18 Edward T. Hall (1959), note 9 above, at page 30.

19 Dean Barnlund, note 4 above, at pages 191-192.

20 Edward T. Hall (1976), note 5 above, at page 162.

21 Edward T. Hall (1976), note 5 above, at page 162.

22 Edward T. Hall (1976), note 5 above, at page 164.

23 Donald W. Hendon & Rebecca Angeles Hendon, *World-class negotiating: Dealmaking in the global marketplace*, John Wiley & Sons, New York, 1990, at page 50.

24 William Gudykunst, *Bridging Differences: Effective Intergroup Communication*, Sage Publications, Newbury Park (California) et al, 1991, at pages 60-62.

25 William Gudykunst, note 24 above, at page 13; Dean Barnlund, note 4 above, at pages 190-192.

26 Dean Barnlund, note 4 above, at page 189.

27 William Gudykunst, note 24 above, at page 66.

28 William Gudykunst, note 24 above, at pages 122-125.

29 Edward T. Hall (1976), note 5 above, at page 162.

30 Carley Dodd, *Dynamics of Intercultural Communication*, (second edition), Wm C Brown Publishers, Dubuque (Iowa), 1982, 1987, at page 38.

31 William Gudykunst, note 24 above, at page 44.

32 R. Keesing, 'Theories of Culture' in (1974) 3 *Annual Review of Anthropology* 73 at page 89, quoted in William Gudykunst, note 24 above, at page 44.

33 R. Keesing, note 32 above.

34   Edward T. Hall (1959), note 9 above, at page 20.

35   William Gudykunst, note 24 above, at pages 26-27.

36   Sogyal Rinpoche, *The Tibetan Book of Living and Dying*, Random House, London, 1992, Reprint 1994, at pages 15-27.

37   Carley Dodd, note 30 above, at pages 38-39; Edward T. Hall (1976), note 5 above, at pages 69 and 182.

38   William Gudykunst, note 24 above, at page 87.

39   Edward T. Hall (1976), note 5 above, at page 227.

40   William Gudykunst, note 24 above, at pages 13, 60-61.

41   Hari Bedi, *Understanding the Asian Manager: Working with the movers of the Pacific century*, Allen & Unwin, Sydney, 1991, at page 3.

42   William Gudykunst, note 24 above, at pages 62-63.

43   Edward T. Hall (1976), note 5 above, at pages 57-69; Hari Bedi, note 41 above, at page 21.

44   Formerly Williston Professor of Law at Harvard Law School. Meeting took place at his office in Harvard Law School on 18 June 1993 whilst I was a Visiting Researcher at Harvard Law School during the Summer of 1993.

45   Aaron Beck, *Love is Never Enough*, Harper and Row, New York, 1988, at page 18, quoted in William Gudykunst, note 24 above, at page 31.

46   William Gudykunst, note 24 above, at page 13.

47   Edward T. Hall (1976), note 5 above, at pages 17-18.

48   William Gudykunst, note 24 above, at pages 2 and 5.

49   William Gudykunst, note 24 above, at page 5.

50   Pierre Casse and Surinder Deol, *Managing Intercultural Negotiations: Guidelines for Trainers and Negotiators*, SIETAR International, Washington D. C., 1985, at page 133.

51   Pierre Casse and Surinder Deol, note 50 above, at page 133.

52   Edward T. Hall (1959), note 9 above, at pages 123-125.

53   The event took place during a workshop on 'Accelerated Learning' held in the School of Humanities & Social Sciences, Bond University, Gold Coast, on 1 June 1994.

54   William Gudykunst, note 24 above, at page 2.

55   Edward T. Hall (1976), note 5 above, at page 57.

56   Edward T. Hall (1976), note 5 above, at page 57.

57   Edward T. Hall (1976), note 5 above, at page 57.

58 See the example in note 53 above.

59 Edward T. Hall (1976), note 5 above, at pages 57-58.

60 Edward T. Hall (1966), note 14 above, at page 2.

61 Dean Barnlund, note 4 above, at page 190.

62 Edward T. Hall (1976), note 5 above, at page 69.

63 Dean Barnlund, note 4 above, at page 42.

64 Harumi Befu, 'Japan and America: How We See Each Other', United States-Japan Trade Council, 1973, at page 6, quoted in Dean Barnlund, note 4 above, at page 42.

65 Harumi Befu, note 64 above.

66 Chin-ning Chu, *The Asian Mind Game: Unlocking the Hidden Agenda of the Asian Business Culture - A Westerner's Survival Manual*, Rawson Associates, New York, 1991, at pages 173-174; Hajime Nakamura (revised English translation edited by Philip Weiner), *Ways of Thinking of Eastern Peoples: India, China, Tibet, Japan*, University of Hawaii Press, Honolulu, 1971.

67 Cigdem Kagitcibasi, 'Family and Socialization in Cross-Cultural Perspective: A Model of Change' in John Berman (ed), *Nebraska Symposium on Motivation 1989: Cross-Cultural Perspectives*, University of Nebraska Press, Lincoln and London, 1990, at page 145.

68 The name of the village is Paloh in the State of Johore. The Chinese there mainly immigrated from the Province of Fukien in southern China, as did my paternal grandparents.

69 Harry C. Triandis, 'Cross-Cultural Studies of Individualism and Collectivism' in John J. Berman (ed), note 67 above, at pages 73-77.

70 Gordon Redding and Gilbert Wong, 'The Psychology of Chinese Organizational Behaviour' in Michael Bond (ed), *The Psychology of the Chinese People*, Oxford University Press, Hong Kong/Oxford/New York, 1986, at pages 267-295.

71 Harry C. Triandis, note 69 above, at page 77.

72 Research has shown that Australia is one of the most individualistic cultures of the world: G. Hofstede, *Culture's Consequences*, Sage, Beverly Hills (California), 1980; Harry C. Triandis, note 69 above, at page 44.

73 Harry C. Triandis, note 69 above, at page 77.

74 Cigdem Kagitcibasi, note 67 above, at page 145.

75   Gordon Redding and Gilbert Wong, note 70 above, at page 285.

76   Gordon Redding and Gilbert Wong, note 70 above, at page 285.

77   He points out that the relative emphasis may depend on two major determinants, i.e. cultural complexity and affluence: see Harry C. Triandis, note 69 above, at page 44.

78   Harry C. Triandis, note 69 above, at page 42.

79   Harry C. Triandis, note 69 above, at page 42.

80   Yigang Pan and Wilfred R. Vanhonacker, 'Chinese and American Cultures: Value Structure and Family Orientation - An Explorative Study', Euro-Asia Centre Research Series, Fontainebleau, September 1992.

81   William Gudykunst, note 24 above, at page 46.

82   Harry C. Triandis, note 69 above, at pages 47 and 87.

83   Harry C. Triandis, note 69 above, at page 81.

84   Harry C. Triandis, note 69 above, at page 53.

85   Harry C. Triandis, note 69 above, at page 53.

86   Triandis recalls the incident whereby Japanese prisoners-of-war during World War II offered to spy for the United States and turned out to be excellent spies for 'once they had changed ingroup, having been taken prisoner against the explicit instructions of their superiors, they no longer defined the self as Japanese': see Harry C. Triandis, note 69 above, at page 81.

87   Harry C. Triandis, note 69 above, at page 87.

88   William Gudykunst, note 24 above, at page 45.

89   See generally, Geert Hofstede, *Cultures and Organizations*, HarperCollins*Publishers*, London, 1994.

90   Geert Hofstede, note 89 above, at pages 4-6.

91   William Gudykunst, note 24 above, (1994 second edition), at page 43.

92   Harry C. Triandis, note 69 above, at page 57.

93   Yigang Pan and Wilfried R. Vanhonacker, note 80 above, at page 3.

94   Harry C. Triandis, note 69 above, at page 43; Michael Bond and Kwang-Kuo Hwang, 'The Social Psychology of Chinese People' in Michael Bond (ed), note 70 above, at pages 221 and 227.

95   Francis L. K. Hsu, note 17 above, at page 135.

96   Harry C. Triandis, note 69 above, at page 44.

97   Francis L.K,. Hsu, note 17 above, at page 88.

98   Michael Bond and Kwang-kuo Hwang, note 94 above, at pages 214-216.

99   *Chung-Yung* , or *The Doctrine of the Mean*, XX:8; Michael Bond and Kwang-Kuo Hwang, note 94 above, at page 216; Tu Wei-ming, *Centrality and Commonality: An Essay on Confucian Religiousness*, State University of New York Press, Albany, 1989, at page 54.

100   Gordon Redding and Gilbert Wong, note 70 above, at page 287.

101   Harry C. Triandis, note 69 above, at pages 45 and 61.

102   Harry C. Triandis, note 69 above, at pages 54-55.

103   Harry C. Triandis, note 69 above, at page 61.

104   David Hall and Roger Ames, *Thinking Through Confucius*, State University of New York Press, 1987, at page 23; Dean Barnlund, note 4 above, at page 38.

105   Edward de Bono, *Serious Creativity*, HarperCollins, London, 1992, at page 32; see also page 40; Edward de Bono, *Conflicts: A Better Way to Resolve Them*, Harrap, London, 1985, at page 21.

106   Tenzin Gyatso, the Fourteenth Dalai Lama of Tibet, *Freedom in Exile : The Autobiography of His Holiness the Dalai Lama of Tibet*, Hodder & Stoughton, London, 1990, at page 99. His Holiness nevertheless disagreed that the Chinese could hope to establish relationships just by eating together.

107   Michael Bond and Kwang-Kuo Hwang, note 94 above, at page 221.

108   Francis L. K. Hsu, note 17 above, at page 304.

109   Harry C. Triandis, note 69 above, at page 45.

110   See the Concise Oxford Dictionary.

111   William Gudykunst, note 24 above, at page 93; Edward T. Hall and Mildred Reed Hall, note 1 above, at page 147.

112   Edward T. Hall and Mildred Reed Hall, note 1 above, at page 147; Harry C. Triandis, note 69 above, at pages 44, 52 and 59.

113   William Gudykunst, note 24 above, at page 45; Dean Barnlund, note 4 above, at page 37.

114   A. Waterman, *The Psychology of Individualism*, Praeger, New York, 1984, at pages 4-5, quoted in William Gudykunst, note 24 above, at pages 45-46.

115   Cigdem Kagitcibasi, note 67 above, at page 155.

116   Ralph Waldo Emerson, *Selected Essays*, Penguin Books, New

York, 1982, at page 178.

[117]   Dean Barnlund, note 4 above, at page 37.

[118]   Dean Barnlund, note 4 above, at page 44.

[119]   William Gudykunst, note 24 above, at pages 46–47.

[120]   Harry C. Triandis, note 69 above, at page 58.

[121]   Harry C. Triandis, note 69 above, at page 58.

[122]   D Bell, *The Cultural Contradictions of Capitalism*, Basic Books, New York, 1976, at page 16, quoted in Harry C. Triandis, note 69 above, at page 101.

[123]   Dean Barnlund, note 4 above, at page 41.

[124]   Harry C. Triandis, note 69 above, at page 43.

[125]   Donald Hendon and Rebecca Hendon, note 23 above, at page 49.

[126]   Francis L. K. Hsu, note 17 above, at page 135; Michael Bond and Kwang-Kuo Hwang, note 94 above, at page 241; Dean Barnlund, note 4 above, at page 41.

[127]   Francis L. K. Hsu, note 17 above, at page 307.

[128]   Harry C. Triandis, note 69 above, at page 84; Dean Barnlund, note 4 above, at pages 37-38.

[129]   Harry C. Triandis, note 69 above, at pages 51 and 54.

[130]   Francis L. K. Hsu, note 17 above, at pages 308-309.

[131]   Dean Barnlund, note 4 above, at page 43.

[132]   Francis L. K. Hsu, note 17 above, at pages 308-309; Edward T. Hall (1966), note 14 above, at page 152.

[133]   William Gudykunst, note 24 above, at pages 45 and 50; Michael Bond and Kwang-Kuo Hwang, note 94 above, at page 222.

[134]   Han Suyin, *My House Has Two Doors (China: Autobiography, History, Book 4)*, Triad Grafton Books, London, 1980 (Reprint 1988), at page 327.

[135]   William Gudykunst, note 24 above, at pages 32-34.

[136]   Edward T. Hall (1976), note 5 above, at page 90.

[137]   Edward T. Hall (1976), note 5 above, at page 86.

[138]   William Gudykunst, note 24 above, at pages 50-51.

[139]   William Gudykunst, note 24 above, at page 96.

[140]   William Gudykunst, note 24 above, at page 96.

[141]   William Gudykunst, note 24 above, at pages 96-97.

[142]   William Gudykunst, note 24 above, at page 95.

[143]   William Gudykunst, note 24 above, at pages 95-96.

[144]   Edward T. Hall (1976), note 5 above, at page 91.

145 Edward T. Hall (1976), note 5 above, at page 91; William Gudykunst, note 24 above, at page 50; Harry C. Triandis, note 69 above, at page 91; Yigang Pan and Wilfried R. Vanhonacker, note 80 above, at page 3.

146 A statement by Harry Triandis, quoted in William Gudykunst, note 24 above, at page 50.

147 William Gudykunst, note 24 above, at page 51; Chin-ning Chu, note 66 above, at page 241.

148 Edward T. Hall (1976), note 5 above, at page 113.

149 Edward T. Hall (1976), note 5 above, at page 91.

150 Edward T. Hall (1976), note 5 above, at page 91; William Gudykunst, note 24 above, at page 51.

151 Donald Levine, *The Flight From Ambiguity*, University of Chicago Press, Chicago, 1985, at page 28, quoted in William Gudykunst, note 24 above, at page 51.

152 Harry C. Triandis, note 69 above, at page 91.

153 Francis L. K. Hsu, note 17 above, at page 141.

154 Francis L. K. Hsu, note 17 above, at pages 6-7; Edward T. Hall (1959), note 9 above, at page 91.

155 Edward T. Hall (1959), note 9 above, at page 37.

156 Edward T. Hall (1959), note 9 above, at page 37.

157 Edward T. Hall (1959), note 9 above, at pages 93-97.

158 Comment made by Professor Roger Fisher, note 44 above.

159 William Gudykunst, note 24 above, at page 94.

160 Harry C. Triandis, note 69 above, at page 60.

161 Donald Hendon and Rebecca Hendon, note 23 above, at page 32.

162 Chin-ning Chu, note 66 above, at page 243.

163 Edward T. Hall (1976), note 5 above, at page 65.

164 Dean Barnlund, note 4 above, at page 43.

165 Harry C. Triandis, note 69 above, at page 60.

166 Jacques Rogot, *Negotiating: From Theory to Practice*, MacMillan, Hong Kong, 1991, at page 33.

167 Edward T. Hall (1976), note 5 above, at page 68.

168 Edward T. Hall (1959), note 9 above, at page xvii.

169 See Roger Fisher and Scott Brown, *Getting Together: Building Relationships As We Negotiate*, Penguin Books, 1988; William Gudykunst, note 24 above, at pages 135-149.

170 Example given by Professor Roger Fisher, note 44 above.

171   Chin-ning Chu, note 66 above, at page 245; Bill Scott, *The Skills of Negotiating*, Gower, Aldershot (Hampshire), 1981, Reprinted 1989, at page 171.

172   Lucian Pye, *Chinese Negotiating Style: Commercial Approaches and Cultural Principles*, Quorum Books, New York et al, 1992, at page 110.

173   Jeffrey Z. Rubin and Frank E.A. Sander, 'Culture, Negotiation and the Eye of the Beholder' (1991) *Negotiation Journal* 249, at page 253.

174   Note 44 above.

175   Joel P. Bowman and Tsugihiro Okuda, 'Japanese American Communication: Mysteries, Enigmas and Possibilities' in (1985) 4 *The Bulletin of the Association for Business Communication*, at page 21, quoted in Robert O. Joy, 'Cultural and Procedural Differences that Influence Business Strategies and Operations in the People's Republic of China' (1989) 54 *Advanced Management Journal*, at page 29.

176   Harry C. Triandis, note 69 above, at page 105.

177   An old Chinese proverb adapted from Lao Tzu's *Tao Te Ching* : see Thomas Cleary (trans. & ed.), *Mastering the Art of War*, Shambhala, Boston & London, 1989, at page 3.

178   Donald Hendon and Rebecca Hendon, note 23 above, at pages 53-54; William Gudykunst, note 24 above, at pages 66-67.

179   William Gudykunst, note 24 above, at pages 64-66.

180   William Gudykunst, note 24 above, at page 44.

3 The Homocentric Chinese

Introduction

Tradition persists to the present, and the present cannot be adequately understood without a knowledge of the past.[1] Contemporary behaviour is often an accumulation of our cultural legacy.[2] In the case of the Chinese, this observation cannot be more true.[3] This is due to the fact that the Chinese, since ancient times, have been accustomed to the precepts of conformance and compliance, stability and security.[4] Resistance to change seems to be more entrenched in Chinese culture than in Western culture. This may be attributable to their respective value norms. For example, the Chinese (Confucian) concept of familism inculcates one with a sense of obedience, loyalty and steadfastness which, in turn, reinforces the characteristic of immobility. Such immobility is manifest in the Chinese outlook towards life generally, for instance, in their unwillingness or reluctance to change residence or employment. Change is not encouraged, innovation little known, and, creativity suppressed.[5] By way of contrast, these very traits of change, innovation and creativity are the qualities of individualism. In a collectivist system, such qualities give way to norms of constancy and continuance. As Hall and Ames remark, 'The actions of individuals who dare to stand away from and challenge tradition and the visions of the past are interpretable by the Confucian as consequences of self-serving effrontery in the face of the legitimate continuities of a received tradition.'[6] This may go to explain why the material progress of China has stagnated though Chinese civilization is an ancient one (believed to be the oldest in the world)[7] and, during the sixteenth century, regarded as superior to Western civilization.[8]

To an interested observer, Chinese culture is a fascinating one.[9] From the Western viewpoint, insights into Chinese culture can help enhance the communication process, particularly in a cross-cultural setting,[10] and also help the Westerner appreciate his or her own culture better as knowledge of another's culture can help one become more aware of one's own culture.[11] In the words of Hall and Hall:

> Only when we can see that there is more than one approach to life and many different ways of behaving can we begin to experience the strong, pervasive influence of our own culture.[12]

After all, 'it is precisely this recognition of differences that provides an opportunity for mutual enrichment by suggesting alternative responses to problems that resist satisfactory solution within a single culture'.[13]

It may be said that the relational nature of Chinese-style negotiation is chiefly influenced by the Chinese way of life: their philosophies, customs, and their perceptions of law, justice and dispute settlement. An understanding of these salient features can help Western negotiators discover the reasons why the Chinese behave the way they do, and go some way towards unveiling their homocentric character.

Philosophies

An examination of traditional Chinese thought can only be undertaken from the Classical Age in China, i.e., the Spring & Autumn and Warring States Periods (770 - 221 B.C.)[14] as until then, in ancient China, proper records were not kept.[15] In addition, these periods witnessed the surge of the philosophic time of the 'Hundred Schools', a time in which scholars were eager to advise a morally declining bureaucracy.[16]

The principal streams of traditional Chinese thinking may be said to be Confucianism, Taoism, Mohism and Legalism.[17] Of the four, Confucianism and Taoism have had lasting significance till today.[18] Cotterell keenly observes that the traditionalist Chinese is a Confucian in public and a Taoist in private.[19]

These Chinese philosophies, particularly Confucianism and Taoism, appear to endow the Chinese with a universalistic view of life, and point out ways to them of the art of living, without inculcating in the Chinese the sense of a divine Creator. Rather, the Chinese belief is one based on the trinity of Heaven, Earth and Humanity. 'In fact, the lack of a creation myth is not only a prominent feature of Confucian symbolism but also a defining characteristic of Chinese cosmology.'[20] Such a philosophic view contrasts sharply with the Western Judeo-Christian tradition, in whose tradition the Universe is deemed the creation and the domain of God, and the way towards reaching God is through adopting the Christian faith alone.[21] The Western worldview is thus seen as one tending towards the exclusivity of a particular faith and the intolerance of polytheism in comprehending the Universe.[22] On the other hand, the Chinese tradition, in its pragmatic and areligious outlook, never poses the question of choosing and abiding by one faith alone.[23] It is for this reason that Chinese culture is considered to be one that tends to include and accommodate and integrate. It is not surprising to find a Chinese professing to be a Confucian, a Taoist *and* a Buddhist all at once.[24] To cite Koller: 'Rather than seeking truth by excluding various alternative views as false, Chinese thought has tended to look for truth in the combination of partially true views. This leads to a spirit of synthesis and harmony which results in tolerance and sympathy.'[25] Such an attitude may account towards the stability of the Chinese civilization over the ages with its tendency to absorb, rather than compete against, other philosophic influences, thereby contributing to its cultural tradition. Cotterell refers to this Chinese trait as the 'astonishing instance of the integrative and absorptive power of Chinese culture'.[26]

Confucianism

Confucius was the man who founded the School of thought which has come to be widely known as Confucianism. The name 'Confucius' is the Latinized version of 'Kung Fu-tzu', meaning 'Master Kung'. He was said to have lived around the period 551-479 B.C..[27]

Classical and contemporary Chinese literature predominates with philosophical discourse on Confuciansim. It may be observed that from ancient times to the present, Confucianism has been the most pervasive influence in Chinese thought: "if we were to describe in one word the Chinese way of life for the last two thousand years, the word would be 'Confucian'".[28]

The Confucianist insistence on proper ritual and correct ceremony known as 'li ' is rooted in the belief of the cosmology of Heaven, Earth and Humanity. For example, the first chapter of *Chung-Yung (Doctrine of the Mean)*[29] reads:

> What Heaven imparts to [one] is called human nature. To follow human nature is called the way. Cultivating the Way is called teaching. The Way cannot be separated from us for a moment. What can be separated from us is not the Way. Therefore the profound [one] is cautious over what [one] does not see and apprehensive over what [one] does not hear. There is nothing more visible than what is hidden and nothing more manifest than what is subtle. Therefore the profound [one] is watchful over [oneself] when [one] is alone. Before the feelings of pleasure, anger, sorrow, and joy are aroused it is called centrality. When the feelings are aroused and each and all attain due measure and degree, it is called harmony. Centrality is the great foundation of the world, and harmony is its universal path. To cultivate centrality and harmony with thoroughness is the way to bring heaven and earth to their proper place and all things their proper nourishment.[30]

The traditionalist Chinese, therefore, believe in the inter-relatedness of all things, and that the Universe exists in an 'unbroken continuum'.[31] Humanity must act with kindness and benevolence towards one another. Otherwise, there would be discord. In this worldview, a disturbance of the social order will similarly upset the total cosmic order.[32] Tu refers to this aspect of Confucianism as an 'anthropocosmic idea'[33] and says thus: 'Humanity is Heaven's form of self-disclosure, self-expression and self-realization. If we fail to live up to our humanity, we fail cosmologically in our mission as co-creator of Heaven and Earth and morally in our duty as fellow participants in the great cosmic transformation'.[34]

It can thus be seen that in the Confucianist view, natural harmony is reflected in humanity's moral goodness. From young, a person ought to be taught the value of moral character so as to act in accordance with cosmic harmony. It is important to cultivate one's virtues and the way to do so is through education: 'A piece of jade cannot become an object of art without chiselling, and a person cannot come to know the moral law without education.'[35] Hence the Chinese emphasis on the role of education.

'*Li*,' commonly translated as 'rites, etiquette, ritual',[36] really refers to propriety. 'It is the courtesy that is essential for a cultured person, and even today the Chinese regard good manners as a sign of moral character.'[37] The Confucianist ethical morality recommends the following: that as between the emperor and his subject, the emperor must act with politeness towards the subject and the subject must be devoted to the ruler; that as between the father and the son, the father must be benign towards the son and the son must be filial to the father; that as between the older brother and the younger brother, the older brother must be amiable towards the younger brother and the younger brother must respect his older brother; that as between the husband and wife, the husband must be gracious towards his wife and the wife must obey her husband; and that as between friends, they must be sincere and trustworthy with one another.[38] These five cardinal sets of relationships represent the cornerstone of the Confucian governance of human affairs.[39] They are seen in this structurally hierachical order, providing a functionally set pattern of socio-political relationships, and more importantly, giving rise to the time-tested principle of reciprocity.

The principle of *li* recognises the existence of social hierachy as a result of humanity being born unequal in 'intelligence and virtue'.[40] Above all, it underlines the Confucian belief of human inter-dependence, inter-relatedness and inter-connectedness. Without appropriate interaction, there would be disharmony and chaos. The way to such interaction lies in the correct observance of propriety. *Li* is thus 'best expressed as approved patterns of behaviour between individuals standing in a definite relationship to each other, and in conformance with a definite system of values relating to such definite relationships'.[41]

Apart from correct behaviour in a set relationship, other important virtues sought to be inculcated are the concepts of filial piety (*hsiao*) , benevolence (*jen*) and righteousness (*yi*).

As we have seen, of the five cardinal relationships advocated by Confucius, three are found within the family system. In Confucianism, the family is the foundation of the larger social and political order. When an individual within the family behaves according to propriety, the family will be correct, proper and right. When each family behaves accordingly, the state will also be correct, proper and right. And when each state so behaves, all under Heaven will be correct, proper and right. The way to achieve this is for each actor to perform the duties and obligations inherent in the five cardinal relationships.[42]

Thus, the practice of filial piety within a family becomes a mandatory Confucian precept. Confucius himself defined *hsiao* to be: 'that parents, when alive, should be served according to propriety; that, when dead, they should be buried according to propriety, and that they should be sacrificed to according to propriety.'[43] One is bound to the duty of honouring the family by displaying scholastic brilliance or acquiring economic wealth, thus enhancing the parents' name. One must also practise ancestral worship. As remarked by Johnston:

> 'Ancestor worship' has a practical and utilitarian as well as a religious or spiritual aspect, and is consciously and deliberately maintained as a method whereby a Chinese

family not only shows its reverence or respect for its departed forefathers but also maintains the continuity of its traditions, strengthens its ties with its scattered members and collateral branches, and safeguards the material interests of its descendants.[44]

The virtue of *hsiao* therefore demands physical, emotional and spiritual fulfilment.[45] Above all, it embodies the requirement of reverence.[46] Once when asked by a student on the subject of filial piety, Confucius replied: 'Nowadays a filial son is just a man who keeps his parents in food. But even dogs or horses are given food. If there is no feeling of reverence, wherein lies the difference ?'[47]

Benevolence is a dominant concept in Confucian philosophy.[48] Benevolence refers to human-heartedness. In this respect, the Master said: 'Benevolence is more vital to the common people than even fire and water. In the case of fire and water, I have seen men die by stepping on them, but I have never seen any man die by stepping on benevolence'.[49] In Mandarin, benevolence is pronounced as *jen* and the word 'person' (referring to humanity) carries a similar pronunciation. In transliteration, the concept of benevolence in *Chung-Yung* (*Doctrine of the Mean*) reads: '*jen* is *jen*'. The pun is apparently intended to be deliberate, 'for to Confucianists, the virtue of humanity is meaningless unless it is involved in actual human relationships.'[50] The following Confucian principle represents a constituent part of the concept of *jen* : 'Do not impose on others what you yourself do not desire'.[51]

Yi, righteousness, is not to be mistaken for 'rights' or 'principles' in Western philosophy.[52] The concept of righteousness is tied in with the communal good, mutual interests, and social goodwill. What is considered righteous is borne out in doing what one is morally obliged to do, in an unconditional and absolute way, for the purpose of the preservation of social harmony.[53] Righteousness means performing one's duty.[54] Righteous conduct lies in doing what is considered good or appropriate by others, not what one considers it to be. For example, one ought to respect and obey one's parents 'because it is morally right and obligatory to do so, and for no other reason'.[55]*Yi*, properly cultivated, therefore enables one to become morally-inclined. It is the medium 'through which one's inner morality becomes properly realized in society ... based on a holistic evaluation of objective conditions'[56], i.e., based not on individual but on overall objective societal perceptions. Put simply, the motivating factor for performing an act is generated from the communal or societal perspective, not from the individual's. In this respect, *Chung-yung (the Doctrine of The Mean)* 'asserts positively that the *common* human experience is the *center* upon which the moral order depends'.[57] In other words, it is the collective centre rather than the centre of the self which should motivate human conduct. This is an indicator of the Chinese orientation towards homocentricity.

The central tenets of Confucianism outlined above all point to the significance of harmony in human relationships. In accordance with Chinese cosmology of Heaven, Earth and Humanity, such harmony in turn integrates humanity with the universe. The norm of harmony is often internalized by the Chinese to the extent that their behaviour is instinctively governed by a desire for peace and concord in inter-personal relationships.[58] As such, the core emphasis on relationships is crucial to our understanding of Chinese conduct. It reveals the Chinese predisposition for inter-personal goodwill. It also enables us to comprehend the Chinese relational approach to negotiation in both philosophical and practical terms.

Taoism

Lao-Tzu, whose name literally means 'Old Master', has been commonly regarded as the founder of Taoism.[59] Said to be born in 604 B.C., his life and his work are hard to trace due to his seclusion and hermitage.[60] What has popularised Taoism is the teaching contained in *Tao Te Ching* (also known as *Lao-tzu*), meaning The Way of Virtue.[61] The main exponents of Taoism are Lao Tzu and Chuang Tzu (350-275 B.C.).[62]

Taoism advocates the nature of being. Nature is the Way,

the *Tao*, and the *Tao* is Nature. Nature should be left alone, and not be subject to any human interference. This means to say that everything has its own *Te*, or virtue, and its own proper nature. It is not for us to impose our value judgements or to seek to modify.[63] It is provided in the Taoist philosophy that: 'A duck's legs, though short, cannot be lengthened without dismay to the duck, and the stork's legs, though long, cannot be shortened without discomfort to the stork. That which is short in nature must not be lengthened and that which is long in nature must not be shortened'.[64]

The Taoists disagree with the Confucian ideal of the cultivation of moral virtue, since this represents an interference with the natural order of things by persuading humanity to conform to a human code of conduct.[65] Everything is best left alone to proceed and develop according to its own nature.

The concept of *rang*, i.e. letting things be, is encapsulated in Lao-Tzu's saying thus: 'The wise man keeps to the deed that consists in taking no action and practises the teaching that uses no words.'[66] The wise person, therefore, subscribes to non-action or non-assertiveness.[67] He or she simply lets things be.

This does not mean that the Taoist philosophy abandons endeavour altogether. In essence, Taoism teaches us to learn from the design and spontaneity, the peace and quietude of nature, and in the process to protect ourselves from our basically self-imposed suffering, harm and anxiety.[68] Such protection derives naturally from keeping away from unnecessary stressful situations. '*Tao* invariably takes no action, and yet there is nothing left undone.'[69] This view allows us to comprehend that Nature runs its own course and that there is no need for us to strive or contrive to achieve things. The great Taoist teaching, therefore, emphasizes being over doing, character over accomplishment, and inaction over action.[70]

Taoism teaches *wu-wei*, literally meaning non-action. However, the more appropriately assigned meaning of non-action or inaction relates to not over-doing things.[71] It means appropriate or necessary activity, or lesser activity or doing less, in order not to defy the Taoist principle of reversal of extremity. 'Reversing is the movement of the *Tao*'.[72] This reversal principle provides that in the natural order of things, when a thing reaches its extreme form, it produces the opposite result. Consider the following Taoist sayings: 'It is upon calamity that blessing leans, upon blessing that calamity rests';[73] 'Diminish a thing and it will increase. Increase a thing and it will diminish';[74] 'Those with little will acquire, those with much will be led astray'.[75] Therefore, according to the principle of reversal, too much of something in itself admits its own harmfulness; and the over-doing of any activity invites its own failure. A famous Chinese story lends support to this view:

> Two men were once competing in drawing a snake; the one who would finish his drawing first would win. One of them, having indeed finished his drawing, saw that the other man was still far behind, so decided to improve it by adding feet to his snake. Thereupon the other man said: 'You have lost the competition, for a snake has no feet'.[76]

Further, in order for one to just be, or let things be, one has to acknowledge the fact that one's changing fortunes are a result of the natural order of things, and so be unperturbed by the notions of luck and adversity. The following parable of the 'Old Man at the Fort' provides an insightful illustration:

> An Old Man was living with his son at an abandoned fort on the top of a hill, and one day he lost a horse. The neighbors came to express their sympathy for his misfortune, and the Old Man asked 'How do you know this is bad luck ?' A few days afterwards, his horse returned with a number of wild horses, and his neighbors came again to congratulate him on this stroke of fortune, and the Old Man replied, 'How do you know this is good luck ?' With so many horses around, his son began to take to riding, and one day he broke his leg. Again the neighbors came around to express their sympathy, and the Old Man replied, 'How do you know this is bad luck ?' The next year, there was a war, and because the Old Man's son was crippled, he did not have to go to the front.[77]

Taoism also reveals to us the utility of the useless. In Chapter 4 of *Chuang-tzu*, a sacred oak had been spared the axe because its wood was of no use. It came to someone's dream and said: 'For a long time I have been learning to be useless. There were several occasions on which I was nearly destroyed, but now I have succeeded in being useless, which is of the greatest use to me. If I were useful, could I have become so great ?'[78] The same Chapter goes on to provide: 'The world knows only the usefulness of the useful, but does not know the usefulness of the useless'.[79]

Essentially, Lao Tzu 'urges a simple and harmonious life, a life in which the profit motive is abandoned, cleverness discarded, selfishness eliminated, and desires reduced'.[80] When one realizes the *Tao*, one becomes one with the universe, thus achieving peace and harmony.[81]

Taoism differs from Confucianism in the sense that the former seeks Nature as the state of being while the latter seeks the cultivation of Humanity as the state of being.[82] They, however, are similar in the belief of the inter-relatedness of Nature and Humanity, and the significance of the attainment of harmony.[83] Very much like Confucianism, Taoist philosophy conveys to and continues for the Chinese their relational aspect of behaviour.

Mohism

Not much is known about the life and writings of Mo Tzu (479-438 B.C.), the founder of Mohism. It is said that his doctrines vanished in 213 B.C. after the suppression of the Hundred Schools by the First Emperor.[84] Nevertheless, some of his precepts have become integrated and have continued to be passed on as a way of life for the Chinese.[85]

Mo Tzu's doctrines premise upon human equality and universal love. Human happiness is to be measured in utilitarian terms.[86] Wars and acts of aggression are despised.[87] A person ought to learn the meaning of sacrificial love and to cultivate the ability to endure any hardship, adversity or misery in the salvation of others.[88]

Cotterell observes that Mo Tzu's gift to the contemporary world is his 'interest in the technical rather than the moral side of state craft'.[89]   Mo Tzu likened the government to a machine, and he sought ways to improve its performance. He warned the bureaucrary against the use of force, and that force should only be applied in defence, not attack.[90]

He was genuinely disturbed by the sufferings of the common people and the inability of the bureaucrary to alleviate their sufferings. He, therefore, advocated compassion as the basis of universal love, a love unrestricted by family ties or connections, encompassing strangers.[91] His popular slogan came to be known as 'promote general welfare and remove evil'.[92]

One can, therefore, analyse the Mohist conception of universal love as furthering the Chinese orientation towards homocentricity. One's actions are to be guided not by self-interest, but to spring from a desire to achieve the common good. The ideal of love for humanity can be said to be yet another reinforcer of the Chinese relational tendencies.

Legalism

Legalism broke the relational mould in China, but a discussion of it is essential because it indirectly reinforced, through its abhorrent nature to the Chinese, the need for people to have faith and trust in each other without resorting to legal, man-made, means.

Confronted with a continual moral decline of the bureaucracy, it became apparent that a shift of philosophic thought towards a system of punishments in governing human behaviour would come to be considered more efficacious than any moral rectifier. The Legalists believed that human nature was basically evil, and thus required the authority of laws and the state.[93] Legalism, therefore, arose in China, a product of the political chaos of the fourth and third centuries B. C.. Its founder, Han Fei Tzu (233 B. C.) remarked:

In ruling the world, one must act in accordance with

human nature. In human nature there are the feelings of liking and disliking, and hence rewards and punishments are effective. When rewards and punishments are effective, interdicts and commands can be 'established', and the way of government is complete.[94]

The Legalists capitalized on the inconsistency of human nature, and claimed that no more than ten persons would do good of their own volition. Laws were, therefore, necessary to ensure that the people could do no wrong.[95] The Confucian emphasis on ethical norms and moral precepts meant little to the Legalists, or the *Fa Chia*. They left the province of morality entirely to the concern of the moralists who could spend time in exerting moral influence: 'a sage ruler relied upon law, not upon wisdom'.[96] They sought to implement laws 'by the most certain processes, the most direct methods, and within the shortest periods of time'.[97]

Fa, or law, was defined to mean 'that which is recorded in the register, set up in the government offices, and promulgated upon the people'.[98] A system of law and punishment was imposed upon the subjects. Emphasis lay in fixed standards externally imposed, as contrasted with the Confucianist emphasis on personal ethics in government.[99] The Legalists subscribed to the view that 'a fixed body of law, impartially and firmly administered, will not fluctuate as does the character of princes'.[100] Subordination to authority for the purpose of strengthening the power of the state ran counter to the Confucianist view that the end of good government was the promotion of the well-being of the subjects and the preservation of social harmony. To them, social harmony could only be achieved through rigid laws.[101]

Historical records show that the Legalists were responsible for establishing the dictatorship of the Chin Dynasty (221-206 B. C.), for unifying China in 221 B. C., and for imposing the most stringent control of life and thought in Chinese History.[102] During the period between 213-212 B. C., books were burned and scholars buried alive.[103] It is no surprise that the supremacy of the Chin Dynasty was shortlived. The Chinese grew in fearful terror of this dynastic period and since then, have rejected the ruthlessness of the Legalists.[104] Legalism was considered 'a regrettable necessity',[105] and 'indicative of a serious moral decline'.[106]

Paradoxically, one may analyse the Legalist School as bequeathing a non-legalistic tradition to the Chinese.[107] This is due to the implicit ills perceived by the Chinese in the Legalist ways of doing things, of administering power, and of their thinking that external enforcement is preferred to moral persuasion.[108] Traditionalist Chinese tend to accept the Confucian approach in human interaction by focussing on social harmony, and are appalled by the Legalist lack of moral comprehension and disintegration of human relationships by placing primacy on rules, not the people. As Lu Chia said: 'Law is used to punish the evil, not to encourage the good. The law is able to punish [the people], but unable to make [the people] uncorrupt; it is able to kill [the people] but unable to make [the people] kind.'[109] Such an aversion to law has led Bodde and Morris to remark that the Chinese 'insistence upon the moral and political dangers involved in the public promulgation of legal norms'[110] is unique and has 'no real parallel in any other civilization.'[111]

Further, the Chinese cosmology of Heaven, Earth and Humanity precludes the notions of a pre-ordained law or a personal divine law-giver.[112] Unlike in the West, the Chinese have not developed a scientific outlook towards law.[113]

In the final analysis, it may be said that Legalism is opposite to the Chinese relational style of behaviour. Hence its rejection. Many Chinese proverbs bear testimony to such a rejection: for instance, 'Inform against a man once and three generations of his family will become your enemies'; 'Let householders avoid litigation, for once go to law and there is nothing but trouble'; 'It is better to die of starvation than to become a thief; it is better to be vexed to death than to bring a lawsuit'.[114]

Customs

The newcomer to Chinese culture is almost always beguiled by the variety of customs practised by the people who boast a great civilization behind them. Some of these customs have been practised with modification by the Chinese in the different provinces in China as well as in their respective adoptive countries.[115] In keeping with the philosophy of this book, it would, perhaps, be best to survey customs from a traditional viewpoint, devoid of modern day interpretations. This is for the purpose of focussing on the predominantly relational character of the Chinese, and avoiding having to deal with modern influences such as individualism or feminism which may have begun to produce an impact on traditional Chinese culture.

Chinese customs can best be seen within the context of the celebration or observance of events or festivals.[116] And the Chinese have a great number of occasions or festive seasons diligently observed year after year. Festivity, an occasion for rejoicing, is also an occasion to worship the ancestors in accordance with the Confucian tradition. The proper person to conduct the ritual and the ceremony is the son. Sumptuous food is proffered to appease the spirits of the ancestors, together with the burning of sacred paper-money in their honour as the prayers are uttered.[117] When the burnt sacred paper-money turns to ash, the son has to return to the ancestral altar to continue praying. The way to discover if the ancestral spirits have been appeased is by tossing two coins. If the tossed coins show a head and a tail, it means that the ancestral spirits have been propitiated. If not, the tossing will repeatedly continue until the coins produce the desired result.[118] Once propitiated, the food offerings can then be cleared from the altar, leaving only the incense to continue to be burnt in honour of the ancestors.[119]

The above description of ancestral worship is evident on festive occasions, and operates as a reminder to the Chinese of the inter-connectedness between the material world and the spiritual world. Such an inter-dependent worldview continues to underline the meaning of relationships - cosmologically between Nature and Humanity, between the dead and the living, and practically between the living and the living.[120] In other words, the worship of one's ancestors symbolically links the relationships between the spiritual and the human worlds, and continues to bring the existing family members together.[121]

It would be useful to showcase certain salient customs[122] and their continuing contribution to the moulding of the homocentric Chinese.

Birth

The birth of a newborn is an occasion to rejoice. The addition to the family is viewed as a gift from Heaven, particularly if the baby is a son.[123] Mencius[124] was quoted as saying, 'there are three things which are unfilial and to have no posterity is the greatest of them.'[125] Here, posterity means a male offspring.[126] Thus, when a Chinese mother gives birth to a son, she is usually surrounded by well-wishing folk who come to praise and congratulate the family for their 'good life', i.e. their fortune in begetting a son.[127] To the Chinese, the arrival of an infant boy therefore bears special significance: he is the one to preserve and perpetuate the family line and is the one to perform the religious rites in honour of the memory of the ancestors.[128] In this connection, i.e., the birth of a male heir for the purpose of the perpetuation of the family name (i.e. honour) and lineage, marriage is considered a necessary institution.[129] A daughter does not possess the same importance and, upon marriage, is considered as not being part of her immediate family any more.[130] The birth of a female baby, therefore, does not have the same significance as that of a male baby.

Name-giving becomes an important exercise. For the Chinese, giving of names is an art in itself.[131] This is because, it is believed, given the appropriate names, the infants will grow up to bear out the meanings contained in their names. It is the honoured duty of the eldest member of the family to bestow a well-chosen name for the newborn.[132] In some cases, parents may themselves wish to give a certain name to their own offspring but this is only possible after having consulted the eldest member of the family.[133] Otherwise, the new parents will be considered unfilial in their act of disobedience. One therefore sees that authority in the family is appreciated even at birth. In the case of a son, names reflecting qualities such as strength, greatness, scholarliness, or brilliance are commonly chosen. In the case of a daughter, names reflecting femininity such as beauty, flower or name of a flower, or grace tend to be selected.[134]

When the baby is one-month old, he or she is said to have attained 'full moon'. The celebration to mark the baby's full-moon, depending on the economic status of the family, can be grand and include relatives and friends from near and far. This is a time when relatives and friends gather together to congratulate the family. Congratulatory gestures in the giving of gifts is common, especially the giving of jewellery or money contained in red packets. One also notices that the colour red is emphasized in the decoration of the event, for red is considered by the Chinese to be the colour of fortune and happiness.[135]

Marriage

Marriages, regarded as happy and auspicious occasions, are believed to be made in Heaven.[136] In Confucianism, marriage is 'a bond of affection between two surnames. It serves the ancestral temple on the one hand and continues the family line on the other'.[137] Here, the expressions of 'two surnames' and 'ancestral temple' respectively mean two families, and a place 'bristling with spirit tablets arranged with in order of generational seniority, each inscribed with the name of a male ancestor'.[138] In Chinese culture, therefore, marriage is regarded as the duty of the parents (of the bridal couple) to ensure continual lineage.[139] Thus, the traditional Chinese view of marriage is utilitarian only, and quite devoid of personal feelings between the bridal couple.[140] This is why traditionalists practise matched marriages. By way of contrast, in Western culture, marriage is the culmination of a loving relationship between the immediate couple, not the pre-occupation of parents or other family members.[141] In the very traditional and conservative Chinese families where a son has not been begotten, it is deemed appropriate for the husband to take a concubine in the hope of her bearing a son to continue the family lineage.[142] In Chinese culture, a wife is always a wife, and concubines are concubines. A Chinese customary marriage is considered monogamous subject to the right of concubinage.[143] This ignorance has led some to believe that the Chinese are, in Western terms, polygamous.[144]

Most traditional Chinese marriages are preceded by a reference to the Chinese horoscope and other spiritual indicators (for example, oracular consultations at Chinese temples) to determine in advance whether the matrimonial union will prove successful.[145] Anxious parents of the marrying couple seek out experts in Chinese character symbolism who can interpret and decipher the meaning of the 'Eight-Character' of the would-be betrothed.[146] The Eight-Character is derived from the hour, day, month, and year of birth of the potential parties.[147] If the character turns out to be incompatible, both families will cancel the engagement.[148]

It is also customary for the bridegroom to provide a sum of money known as bride-wealth to the bride's family to enable the bride to make some initial purchase. Be that as it may, the bride's family cannot retain any part of such bride-wealth.[149] In fact, in some instances, through the consent of the bride's parents, the bride-wealth may be dispensed with.

Again, the colour red is extensively used in the celebration, to mark the happiness of the occasion and signify the future prosperity of the family.[150] The Chinese normally prefer to have an elaborate wedding, as long as they have the means to do so. An elaborate wedding is indicative of the social status of the family.[151] Wedding invitations are distributed to relatives near and far, the clan associations, prominent members of the community and close friends. Due to the fact that marriage is largely the concern of the family elders, one finds that the majority of the wedding guests tend to be relatives and friends of the parents rather than friends of the bridal couple.[152] The wedding ceremony is, therefore, another example of the Chinese emphasis on relationships.[153]

Funerals

Unlike the occasions of birth and marriage which are considered auspicious, death is not only received with solemnity and sadness, but usually regarded as taboo and associated with bad luck.[154]

In accordance with Confucian tradition, the observance of filial piety in relation to a funeral is paramount.[155] The eldest son, especially, takes charge of the conducting of the funeral, and performs the requisite rites. He is expected, too, to continue a lifetime of ancestral worship. This is consonant with the Confucian precept of *hsiao* inherent in *li*.

The colour associated with mourning has changed over time. In ancient China, white used to be the colour of mourning. However, in Malaysia, for instance, Chinese Malaysians tend to use the colour black. No real account can be given for such a change. What is common, though, is the fact that the mourners are prohibited from wearing attractively-coloured clothing. Such prohibited colours include red, yellow, orange and any shade of these colours. This is because such colours are considered 'happy' colours and therefore inappropriate at a time of sadness. Normally, the mourners tend to use blue, green, white or black colours, which signify solemnity or neutrality.[156]

Chinese New Year Festival

The Chinese view the passing of time in terms of a twelve-year cycle. These twelve years are associated with twelve animals in the following order: rat, ox, tiger, rabbit, dragon, snake, horse, sheep, monkey, rooster, dog and pig.[157] For example, 1996 is the Year of the Rat. Each animal, in a particular year, is said to bear one of the five elements of earth, wood, water, metal or fire. Consequently, each animal cycle takes sixty years to complete.

The Chinese New Year, calculated on the lunar basis, is regarded as the most important annual event. In the Gregorian calendar, the Chinese New Year occurs sometime in January or February, and varies from year to year. The New Year actually begins on the thirtieth day of the twelfth lunar month of the preceding year and continues until the sixteenth day of the first lunar month of the succeeding year. Within this period, the significant days are the thirtieth day of the old year (i.e. New Year's Eve), the first day to the fifth day, and the fifteenth day of the first lunar month.[158] For Chinese originating from different provinces in China, there are particular days which are regarded as specific days of worship. For instance, Chinese Malaysian migrants from the Province of Fukien in southern China observe the ninth day of the first lunar month since this day is considered the birthday of the Emperor of Heaven.[159]

Generally, the celebrations last fifteen days.[160] The eve of the New Year witnesses the traditional family reunion dinner. The scattered family members from afar are obliged, as far as is humanly possible, to return home to partake in the meal. This goes to emphasize the unity of the family.[161]

The Chinese can be said to be generally obsessed with the notion of luck. In this connection, Burkhardt remarks thus: 'The conception of a personal God, Lord and Creator of the Universe, never occurred to the Chinese, but if they have an overriding divinity it is Luck'.[162] Needless to say, in their anxiety to safeguard or attract good luck, the first day of the New Year is fraught with taboos. For instance, brooms are to be hidden from sight and sweeping is not allowed, for this may sweep away the entire year's good luck. Everyone has to remember not to utter any ill word, and take care not to break anything fragile for fear of incurring bad luck.[163]

The colour red is prominently used. Pieces of red cloth are hung in front of doorways to welcome luck and prosperity. Money is contained inside red packets as gifts for children.[164] Family, relatives and friends pay house visits to mark a time of togetherness and foster relationships.

Ching-Ming

Ching-Ming, literally meaning clear and bright, is a time when the living commemorate their dead ones.[165] The Western equivalent would be All Souls' Day. It is observed at any day during the first half of the third lunar month. It is a day when the families and relatives tidy up the graves of the departed, and make sacrificial offerings.[166] This occasion also reinforces the practice of ancestral worship, based on the Confucian cult of filial piety.[167] It has always been a firm belief of the Chinese that their continuing well-being in life is a bestowal of the departed ancestral spirits.[168] As Burkhardt observes, 'Chinese constantly consult the spirits of their ancestors when embarking on a new venture, such as opening a business or building a house'.[169] This is why it is regarded as very important to keep observing the rites and rituals necessary to remind the ancestors that their spiritual welfare is remembered and attended to.

On the social front, the occasion draws family members together, providing them an opportunity for reminiscing. It strengthens long-held family values, and brings the importance of relationships to the forefront.

Dumpling Festival

The origin of this festival can be traceable to the suicidal death of a patriotic poet-minister who sacrificed his own life in order to escape the evil practices of a corrupt government.[170] Legend has it that Ch'u Yuan, a great poet and a minister of the State of Ch'u became disillusioned with the corrupt government of the day. He was subsequently dismissed through palace intrigue and preferred a death of honour rather than to be a corrupt minister himself. He clasped a huge stone with both hands and jumped into the sea in an act of patriotism. Fearing that his body might be eaten by the fish, sympathisers prepared dumplings made of glutinous rice and threw them into the sea as fish food in the hope of luring them away from him.[171]

This Festival, celebrated on the fifth day of the fifth lunar month, in memory of the great poet, is symbolic of the Chinese insistence on the virtues of loyalty and patriotism in governance.[172] The Festival has been popularised with the race of the dragon boats, and is known in modern times as the Dragon Boat Festival.[173]

Hungry Ghosts Festival

We have noted that the Chinese believe the welfare of the spirits is linked to the welfare of human beings on earth. The significance of this Festival lies in this belief and the fact that the well-being of the human world is a favour granted by Heaven pleased with human behaviour. They also venture to think that there are some wandering spirits that may have been forgotten by their living relatives. The hungry ghosts are, as Wong writes: 'the category of neglected shades, who have not been cared for by their living relatives and who are, therefore, prone to be malignant and mischievous.'[174] The month of the hungry ghosts, occuring during the seventh lunar month for it is believed that they are then released from Hell,[175] is therefore a time for the Chinese community to get together to make sacrifical offerings in order to appease these wandering spirits.[176]

The fear that these ghosts may disturb the living is a very real fear among the Chinese, especially among the more superstitious and the wary.[177] As Vaughan puts it, 'during this month the spirits are supposed to wander about the earth and if not propitiated plague the offenders with divers, pains and aches and more serious mishaps'.[178]

Mooncake Festival

Various explanations have been given to trace the origin of the Mooncake Festival.[179] This Festival is celebrated on the fifteenth day of the eighth lunar month, and therefore, is also known as the Mid-Autumn Festival.[180]

This is another occasion to foster close inter-personal relationships.[181] Yet another aim is to achieve harmony between the moon - a manifestation of nature - and humanity.[182] This is done through feasting and rejoicing and paying homage to the ancestors. Gifts of mooncakes are exchanged amongst relatives and friends.[183]

The highlight of the Mooncake Festival is the colourful display of lanterns.[184] Thus, it is also referred to as the Lantern

Festival.

Winter Festival

This festival is celebrated during the last month of the lunar year, and originated in the old agrarian communities in China who rested during the cold winter, and who waited for spring to plant their crops again.[185] The Festival again serves as an occasion for the performance of ancestral worship. Specially-made sweet and colourful marble-shaped rice-balls are served. The round shape, for the Chinese, is symbolic of family unity.[186]

    With the close of the year, the families are again busy making preparations to welcome the new year.

    The foregoing customary practices, passed down from bygone times, point to the continual cultural emphasis on establishing and preserving relationships, in aid of promoting social harmony. With the changing times, it is possible that some of these customary practices may be in place without the participants being consciously aware of their original meaning or significance.[187] Such a lack of awareness notwithstanding, it remains to be said that family occasions and festivities continue to bring family members and friends together and there is, therefore, a constant reminder in practice of the value of relationships and mutual inter-dependence.[188] It is therefore not surprising that Chinese negotiation is, consciously or unconsciously, shaped and influenced by the Chinese relational style of conducting their everyday lives through customary practices. Support for their relational tendency, as has been shown, is also a product of their philosophic outlook.

Perceptions Of Law And Justice And Dispute Settlement

> The thing is we should make it our aim that there not be any law suits at all
> - Confucius, *The Analects*, XII: 13.

The Chinese have been commonly regarded as a non-litigious people. They abhor confrontation, and prefer to let problems iron themselves out rather than deal with the people involved.[189] In this connection, Burkhardt states: 'The Chinese are a smiling race, and have the good sense to accept a compromise rather than nurse resentment for failure to achieve a complete victory. Harmony ranks high among the virtues they admire, and they dread taking an irrevocable step, whose consequences may be unpredictable.'[190]

It may be said that in terms of disputes, the Chinese prefer the dissolution of disputes to a resolution of disputes.[191] This means to say that when a problem is perceived, the people involved work around the problem and attempt to dissipate it. Unlike the Westerners, the Chinese do not tend to confront the people concerning the problem; their tendency is to handle the situation in a delicate way. The intention of the Chinese is to minimize inter-personal conflict and observe social harmony.[192] This comment is especially true where the parties live closely together in a community and continuous daily contact is expected.

Furthermore, the Chinese subscribe to the anthropocosmic conception. Lubman similarly observes that, for the traditional Chinese, 'disputes were viewed as disruptions of the natural harmony which linked individual, group, society, and the entire universe'.[193] A conflict is therefore, perceived not just from a human dimension, but is connected with the intricate cosmic world.[194] A desire not to upset the universe or cause disharmony becomes a pre-occupation with the Chinese. The way to restore harmony is through compromise.[195] In this connection, the virtue of *jang*, which means yielding, is encouraged in order to ward off 'friction and disharmony',[196] in an attempt 'to meet the opponent half-way than to stand on principle'.[197] After all, as Cohen accurately points out, the emphasis of Confucian values is 'not on the rights of the individual but the functioning of the social order'.[198]

We have seen how the Legalist School has been largely rejected by the traditionalist Chinese. As a corollary, the process of dispute settlement among the Chinese points to informal means rather than the formal ones involving the bureaucracy. The bureaucracy (the courts forming a part of it), represents one of the three great taboos for the Chinese: the other two being the undertaker (symbolic of death) and the pawnshop (indicative of indebtedness).[199] The informal means may include the handling of disputes by village elders, clan chiefs, community leaders, or trusted relations.[200] Such disputes usually relate to civil matters, on issues of inheritance, succession or marriage. Criminal prosecutions which are considered beyond private sanctions remain matters for the legal means of enforcement.[201]

The use of informal means suggests that the preferred methods of dispute settlement are mediation and conciliation.[202] Litigation is seen by the Chinese as encouraging the pursuit of one's own interests at the expense of others.[203] Further, litigation runs counter to the Confucian spirit of self-criticism. Whenever one is unreasonably treated by another, one ought, by the process of self-criticism, to regard it as a result of some personal failings on one's part and to seek the source and solution of the problem. It is said that one's attempt at self-improvement may elicit a positive response from the other party and the problem which may otherwise lead to a dispute would thereby be terminated even before it starts. A person who practises self-criticism is considered to be morally disposed, one who does not insist on rights but who prefers to settle a dispute through the means which enable both parties to save personal embarrassment and not to lose face.[204] A lawsuit will cause one to lose face.[205] It also implies a failing in one's virtue and an embarrassment that one does not command sufficient respect from the other to arrive at mutual concessions.[206] Moral persuasion gains precedence over legal method: 'Education and persuasion, not authority or force, must prevail'.[207] For the Chinese, therefore, litigation is considered the last resort.

By way of contrast with the Westerners who are accustomed to perceiving litigation as a first resort in resolving conflicts, in most civil disputes, the Chinese tend to use mediational or conciliatory means of settlement rather than resort to litigation.[208] Seen in this light, litigation becomes the alternative dispute resolution for the Chinese. In a similar vein,

Ting-Toomey, in a cross-cultural study of individualists and collectivists and their strategic differences in approaching a conflict, hypothesizes thus:

> Individualists will be more concerned with saving their own face, autonomy, domination, control, and solutions to the problem; they will use direct negotiation strategies. By contrast, collectivists will be more concerned with saving face for the other or for both, approval, being obliging and smooth, and avoiding conflict. They will use indirect negotiation strategies - for example, they will welcome mediators.[209]

The Chinese, being homocentric and collectivist, are therefore inclined towards a mediational style of resolving conflicts.

Mediation or conciliation encourages open talk. As Roberts says, 'through talk people get to know what others are thinking and are going to do, as well as how their own actions are perceived, and are enabled to arrange their affairs accordingly'.[210] The use of mediation or conciliation is a dispute settlement process whereby a third party assists the disputants in reaching a compromise solution without dictating terms to them.[211] The compromise reached by the parties is often concluded in the partaking of a feast by the mediator, the clan chiefs, and the heads of the disputing families (and sometimes the close friends of the disputants).[212] The feast serves three main functions: firstly, a public testimony of the restoration of goodwill between the disputants and their families; secondly, an opportunity for the offender to recover his or her loss of face as a result of the dispute and to regain membership of the group by 'playing the honourable role of host';[213] and thirdly, a reminder to the community of the importance of preserving social harmony.[214]

Because a conflict has a far more significant social aspect than the personal aspect, acceptable solutions are seen in the offering of tea to the elder member(s) of the vindicated party, in the offering of appropriate materials in the colour red, in the holding of a feast, or in the offering of an apology. Monetary compensation is rarely sought, for it is considered 'undignified'.[215] The Chinese consider it far more important to restore favourable public opinion and regard monetary compensation as an inadequate remedy.[216] Money is relevant if the dispute itself involves actual monetary issues, such as compensation for breakage or damage.

In respect of the Chinese perception of law, justice and dispute settlement, Hsu provides the following excellent summary:

> In the Chinese philosophy, the interpretation of law is based upon human feelings and situations not upon absolute standards. Disputants do not turn to lawyers who argue a client's case in abstract terms joined with appeals to legal precedent. Instead, they look to a middleman or peacemaker. A concept of law that defines justice in human terms has no place for abstract or absolute notions of right and wrong. Each case is different, and it is always right or wrong that is relative: what is right for the father may be wrong for the son, or what is permissible in one situation may be punishable in another. Nor does this relativistic approach stop even here. The Chinese middleman does not uphold one party against another or insist that one is completely right and the other wholly wrong. His mission is to smooth ruffled feelings by having each disputant sacrifice a little, whether the sacrifice involves principles or not.[217]

Conclusion

The participants of any civilization take a long time to change their habits of behaviour.[218] The Chinese, whose traditions date back to more than five thousand years, face the formidable task of adhering to traditional values and adapting to modern norms.[219] The changes, though, have been gradual. Many of the cultural traditions of the Chinese continue to be preserved and practised, albeit with suitable modifications.

The continuing influence of lasting Confucian and Taoist precepts, the perpetuation of salient customary practices, and the enduring aversion to the formal law and justice system, all tend to suggest that the Chinese place primacy on people and on harmony in human interaction, underline their preference for social good and communal well-being, and thus reinforce their homocentricity.

NOTES

1   Benjamin I. Schwartz, *The World of Thought in Ancient China*, The Belknap Press of the Harvard University Press, Cambridge (Massachusetts), 1985, at page 9.

2   See Foreword by J.D. Legge in C. Mary Turnbull, *A Short History of Malaysia, Singapore and Brunei*, Graham Brash, Singapore, 1981.

3   See Arthur Cotterell, *China: A Concise Cultural History*, John Murray, London, 1988, at page xxii; Robert Elegant, *Pacific Destiny: Inside Asia Today*, Hamish Hamilton, London, 1990, at page 273; GOH Bee Chen, *The Traditional Chinese Concept of Law, Justice and Dispute Settlement, with Specific Reference to the Rural Chinese Malaysians*, unpublished Project Paper, Faculty of Law, University of Malaya, Kuala Lumpur, 1982/83.

4   See Francis L. K. Hsu, *Americans and Chinese: Passage to Differences*, University of Hawaii Press, Honolulu, 1981 (3rd edition), at pages 134-137 and 316-320.

5   Edward de Bono, *Conflicts: A Better Way to Resolve Them*, Harrap, London, 1985, at page 22.

6   David Hall and Roger Ames, *Thinking Through Confucius*, State University of New York Press, Albany, 1987, at page 23.

7   Arthur Cotterell, note 3 above, at page xiii.

8   Robert Elegant, note 3 above, at page 502.

9   Richard Wilhelm (Translated from the German text by Irene Eber), *Lectures on the I Ching : Constancy and Change*, Princeton University Press, Princeton, 1979, at page ix.

10   See Edward T. Hall and Mildred Reed Hall, *Understanding Cultural Differences*, Intercultural Press, Inc., Yarmouth (Maine), 1990; Edward T. Hall, *The Silent Language*, Greenwood Press, Publishers, Westport (Connecticut), 1959; Edward T. Hall, *Beyond Culture*, Doubleday, New York, 1976.

11   Edward T. Hall and Mildred Reed Hall, note 10 above, at page 139.

12	Edward T. Hall and Mildred Reed Hall, note 10 above, at page 139.
13	David Hall and Roger Ames, note 6 above, at page 5.
14	Arthur Cotterell, note 3 above, at page 41.
15	(Mandarin text) Parker Po-fei Huang et al, "Lecture Twenty: Philosophy" in *Twenty Lectures on Chinese Culture*, Yale University Press, New Haven and London, 1967, at page 174.
16	Arthur Cotterell, note 3 above, at page 67.
17	Arthur Cotterell, note 3 above, at page 67; Parker Po-fei Huang et al, note 15 above, at pages 174-176.
18	Arthur Cotterell, note 3 above, at page 67.
19	Arthur Cotterell, note 3 above, at page 68.
20	Tu Wei-ming, *Centrality and Commonality: An Essay on Confucian Religiousness*, State University of New York Press, Albany, 1989, at page 69.
21	Tu Wei-ming, note 20 above, at page 9; Francis L.K. Hsu, at page 254.
22	Stig Stromholm, *A Short History of Legal Thinking in the West*, Norstedts, Stockholm, 1985, at page 78; Francis L.K. Hsu, note 4 above, at pages 253-266.
23	Francis L.K. Hsu, note 4 above, at page 265.
24	Francis L.K. Hsu, note 4 above, at pages 254-255; Robert E. Allinson, "An Overview of the Chinese Mind" in Robert E. Allinson (ed.), *Understanding the Chinese Mind*, Oxford University Press, Hong Kong/Oxford/New York, 1989, at page 15. For instance, in my own case, I have grown up in a Confucianist-Taoist-Buddhist family environment, and upon marriage to a sikh, have converted to Sikhism, but I continue to subscribe to all philosophical and religious doctrines.
25	John M. Koller, *Oriental Philosophies*, Charles Scribner's Sons, New York, 1985 (second edition), at page 247.
26	Arthur Cotterell, note 3 above, at page 133.
27	These dates might not have been exact. See Kenneth Scott Latourette, *THE CHINESE, their History and Culture*, MacMillan Company, New York, 1964, at page 54.
28	Wm Theodore de Barry, Wing-tsit Chan and Burton Watson (compl.), *Sources of Chinese Tradition*, Volume I, Columbia University Press, New York, 1960, at page 17.
29	*Chung-Yung*, or the *Doctrine of the Mean*, was originally Chapter 31 of the *Book of Rites*, one of the Confucianist Five Classics. The

Five Classics are: *Book of Change, Book of Poetry, Book of History, Book of Rites and the Spring and Autumn Annals*. For detailed analysis of *Chung-Yung*, see Tu Wei-ming, note 20 above.

30   *Chung-Yung*, I:1-5, quoted in Tu Wei-ming, note 20 above, at pages 5-6. To make the translated text gender neutral, the word '[one]' has been substituted.

31   Derk Bodde and Clarence Morris, *Law in Imperial China*, Harvard University Press, Cambridge (Massachusetts), 1967, at page 4.

32   Derk Bodde and Clarence Morris, note 31 above, at page 4; Tu Wei-ming, note 20 above, at page 102.

33   Tu Wei-ming, note 20 above, at page 102.

34   Tu Wei-ming, note 20 above, at page 102.

35   Confucius, *Book of Rites (Li Chi)*, translated by Lin Yu-tang, *The Wisdom of Confucius*, Random House, Modern Library, New York, 1938, at page 241 quoted in John M. Koller, note 25 above, at page 276.

36   Arthur Cotterell, note 3 above, at page 68.

37   Arthur Cotterell, note 3 above, at page 68.

38   Parker Po-fei Huang et al, note 15 above, at pages 174-176; see also John M. Koller, note 25 above, at page 214.

39   Francis L. K. Hsu , note 4 above, at page 378.

40   Chu T'ung-tsu, *Law and Society in Traditional China*, Mouton & Co., Paris/La Haye, 1961, at page 226.

41   Hu Hsien-Chin (1948) at page 53 quoted in Sybille van der Sprenkel, *Legal Institutions in Manchu China: A Sociological Analysis*, University of London The Athalone Press, London, 1962, at page 31.

42   Francis L. K. Hsu, note 4 above, at page 378.

43   James Legge (trans.), *The Chiness Classics*, (1895) Volume I, at page 147 quoted in H. McAleavy, "Chinese Law in Hong Kong: the Choice of Sources" in J. N. D. Anderson (ed.), *Changing Law in Developing Countries*, George Allen & Unwin Ltd., London, 1963, at page 262; *The Analects*, II:5.

44   R. F. Johnston, *Confucianism and Modern China*, Victor Gollancz Limited, London, 1934, at page 54 quoted in WONG Choon San, *A Cycle of Chinese Festivities*, Malaysia Publishing House Limited, Singapore, 1967, at page 119.

45   John M. Koller, note 25 above, at pages 268-269.

46   John M. Koller, note 25 above, at page 269.

47   *The Analects*, II:7.

48   David Hall and Roger Ames, note 6 above, at page 111.

49   *The Analects*, XV: 35.

50   Wing-tsit Chan (trans. & compl.), *A Source Book in Chinese Philosophy*, Princeton University Press, Princeton, 1963, at page 104; Tu Wei-ming, note 20 above, at page 50.

51   *The Analects*, V: 12; XII: 2; XV: 24.

52   David Hall and Roger Ames, note 6 above, at pages 101-102.

53   David Hall and Roger Ames, note 6 above, at page 103.

54   John M. Koller, note 25 above, at pages 269- 270.

55   John M. Koller, note 25 above, at page 270.

56   Tu Wei-ming, note 20 above, at page 52.

57   Tu Wei-ming, note 20 above, at page 69 (original emphasis by the author).

58   John M. Koller, note 25 above, at pages 3 and 272-273.

59   Arthur Cotterell, note 3 above, at page 76.

60   Arthur Cotterell, note 3 above, at page 76.

61   Arthur Cotterell, note 3 above, at page 76.

62   Arthur Cotterell, note 3 above, at page 76; Parker Po-fei Huang et al, note 15 above, at page 175.

63   Donald A. MacKenzie, *China and Japan*, Bracken Books, London, 1986, Reprint 1992, at page 298.

64   *Chuang-tzu,,* Chapter VIII. Also quoted in Adrian Marshall, "Man and Nature in Malaysia - attitudes to Wildlife and Conservation" in P. A. Scott (ed.), *Man and Nature in Southeast Asia*, School of Oriental and African Studies, University of London, London, 1978, at page 29.

65   Arthur Cotterell, note 3 above, at page 77.

66   Quoted in Arthur Cotterell, note 3 above, at page 77.

67   Arthur Cotterell, note 3 above, at page 77.

68   John M. Koller, note 25 above, at page 284.

69   *Tao Te Ching*, Chapter 37, quoted in John M. Koller, note 25 above, at page 289.

70   Fung Yu-Lan (edited by Derk Bodde), *A Short History of Chinese Philosophy*, MacMillan Company, 1948, at pages 99-101.

71   Fung Yu-Lan, note 70 above, at page 100.

72   *Tao Te Ching*, Chapter 40, quoted in Fung Yu-Lan, note 70 above, at page 97.

73   *Tao Te Ching,* Chapter 58, quoted in Fung Yu-Lan, note 70 above, at page 97.

74   *Tao Te Ching,* Chapter 42, quoted in Fung Yu-Lan, note 70 above, at page 97.

75   *Tao Te Ching,* Chapter 22, quoted in Fung Yu-Lan, note 70 above, at page 97.

76   Fung Yu-Lan, note 70 above, at page 100.

77   By the great Taoist philosopher, Lieh Tzu (fifth century B. C.).

78   Fung Yu-Lan, note 70 above, at page 64.

79   Fung Yu-Lan, note 70 above, at page 64.

80   John M. Koller, note 25 above, at page 253.

81   John M. Koller, note 25 above, at page 285.

82   John M. Koller, note 25 above, at page 284.

83   John M. Koller, note 25 above, at pages 284-285.

84   Arthur Cotterell, note 3 above, at page 68.

85   John M. Koller, note 25 above, at page 254.

86   John M. Koller, note 25 above, at page 254.

87   Wm Theodore de Barry, Wing-tsit Chan and Burton Watson (compl.), note 28 above, at page 67.

88   Parker Po-fei Huang et al, note 15 above, at page 175.

89   Arthur Cotterell, note 3 above, at page 76.

90   Arthur Cotterell, note 3 above, at page 76.

91   Arthur Cotterell, note 3 above, at page 76.

92   John M. Koller, note 25 above, at page 254.

93   John M. Koller, note 25 above, at page 256.

94   Quoted in Fung Yu-Lan, note 70 above, at page 162.

95   Fung Yu-Lan, note 70 above, at page 160.

96   *Kuan-tzu,* 15:4a, quoted in Chu T'ung-tsu, note 40 above, at page 260.

97   Chu T'ung-tsu, note 40 above, at page 261.

98   Fung Yu-Lan, note 70 above, at page 162.

99   William McNeill and Jean Sedlar (ed.), *Classical China,* Oxford University Press, New York, 1960, at page 75.

100   Kenneth Scott Latourette, note 27 above, at page 59.

101   GOH Bee Chen, note 3 above, at page 85.

102   Wing-tsit Chan (trans. & compl.), note 50 above, at page 251.

103   Arthur Cotterell, note 3 above, at page 79.

104   Wing-tsit Chan (trans. & compl.), note 50 above, at page 251;

GOH Bee Chen, note 3 above, at page 87.

105 Jerome Alan Cohen, "Chinese Mediation on the Eve of Modernization" (1966) 54 *California Law Review*, at page 1206.

106 Derk Bodde and Clarence Morris, note 31 above, at page 49.

107 Wing-tsit Chan (trans. & compl.), note 50 above, at page 251.

108 Rene David and John E. C. Brierley, *Major Legal Systems in the World Today*, Stevens & Sons, London, 1985, (third edition), at pages 520-521; GOH Bee Chen, note 3 above, at pages 68-70.

109 Lu Chia (third and second centuries B. C.), quoted by Huan Kuan, *Yen t'ieh lun* 10, 6b-7a, in Chu T'ung-tsu, note 40 above, at page 248.

110 Derk Bodde and Clarence Morris, note 31 above, at page 17.

111 Derk Bodde and Clarence Morris, note 31 above, at page 17.

112 Dennis Lloyd, *The Idea of Law*, Penguin Books, Harmondsworth, 1977, at page 71.

113 Dennis Lloyd, note 112 above, at page 71; GOH Bee Chen, note 3 above, at page 64.

114 See Stanley Lubman, "Mao and Mediation: Politics and Dispute Resolution in Communist China" (1967) 55 *California Law Review* , at page 1296; Sybille van der Sprenkel, note 41 above, at page 135; Jerome Alan Cohen, note 105 above, at pages 1201, 1211-1215.

115 V. R. Burkhardt, *Chinese Creeds and Customs*, South China Morning Post Limited, Hong Kong, 1982, at page 82; See generally Lynn Pan, *Sons of the Yellow Emperor: The Story of the Overseas Chinese*, Mandarin Paperback, London, 1990.

116 V.R. Burkhardt, note 115 above, at pages 1-5.

117 GOH Bee Chen, note 3 above, at page 50; V.R. Burkhardt, note 115 above, at pages 150-152.

118 For instance, in my family, my father continues to observe this practice today.

119 GOH Bee Chen, note 3 above, at page 50.

120 Rene David and John E. C. Brierley, note 108 above, at page 518.

121 Arthur Cotterell, note 3 above, at page 68.

122 In addition to indications as to their sources in the footnotes, the information on Chinese customs is a collection of knowledge passed down to me by my late grandmother (an immigrant to Malaysia in the early twentieth century), and my observations of continuing customary practices in Malaysia and Australia.

123 V. R. Burkhardt, note 115 above, at page 86.

124   A famous disciple of Confucius. See Arthur Cotterell, note 3 above, at page 71; John M. Koller, note 25 above, at page 253.

125   Found in James Legge, note 43 above, at page 313, quoted in H. McAleavy, note 43 above, at pages 262-263.

126   V.R. Burkhardt, note 115 above, at pages 64 and 86.

127   GOH Bee Chen, note 3 above, at page 39.

128   Kenneth Scott Latourette, note 27 above, at pages 568-569; Chu T'ung-Tsu, note 40 above, at page 29.

129   Kenneth Scott Latourett, note 27 above, at pages 568-569.

130   V.R. Burkhardt, note 115 above, at page 87.

131   V.R. Burkhardt, note 115 above, at page 229.

132   GOH Bee Chen, note 3 above, at page 40.

133   V.R. Burkhardt, note 115 above, at page 230.

134   GOH Bee Chen, note 3 above, at page 39.

135   Chin-ning Chu, *The Asian Mind Game: Unlocking the Hidden Agenda of the Asian Business Culture - A Westerner's Survival Manual*, Rawson Associates, New York, 1991, at page 163; V.R. Burkhardt, note 115 above, at page 77; Sarah Rossbach, *Feng Shui*, Century, London et al, 1984, at page 121.

136   V. R. Burkhardt, note 115 above, at page 85.

137   *Li Chi Chu-su*, quoted in Chu T'ung-tsu, note 40 above, at page 91.

138   Lynn Pan, note 115 above, at page 10; see aslo V.R. Burkhardt, note 115 above, at pages 150-152.

139   Chu T'ung-tsu, note 40 above, at page 99; Kenneth Scott Latourette, note 27 above, at page 569.

140   Francis L. K. Hsu, note 4 above, at page 145. Hsu goes on, at page 151, to suggest that from about the beginning of the twentieth century, changes have taken place towards an "emphasis on romantic love and on living away from the husband's parents", but he also indicates that these changes are mainly found in the Western-educated Chinese.

141   Francis L. K. Hsu, note 4 above, at page 145; *Hall v. Wright* 120 E.R. 688, at 695.

142   Francis L. K. Hsu, note 4 above, at pages 101 and 50; H. McAleavy, note 43 above, at pages 262-265; Sybille van der Sprenkel, note 41 above, at page 15; V.R. Burkhardt, note 115 above, at page 87.

143   H. McAleavy, note 43 above, at pages 264-265; Chu T'ung-tsu, note 40 above, at pages 124-125.

144   GOH Bee Chen, note 3 above, at page 102.

145   GOH Bee Chen, note 3 above, at page 48; Ray Nyce (edited by Shirle Gordon), *Chinese New Villages in Malaya: A Community Study*, Malaysian Sociological Institute, Singapore, 1973, at page 33.

146   'Eight Character' here means the unique personal characteristics of the couple to ensure compatibility. See V. R. Burkhardt, note 115 above, at page 81.

147   V. R. Burkhardt, note 115 above, at page 81.

148   V. R. Burkhardt, note 115 above, at page 81.

149   Ray Nyce, note 145 above, at page 35.

150   Chin-ning Chu, note 135 above, at page 163; Sarah Rossbach, note 135 above, at page 121.

151   Francis L.K. Hsu, note 4 above, at pages 314-317.

152   Ray Nyce, note 145 above, at page 36.

153   Francis L.K. Hsu, note 4 above, at pages 316-317.

154   Chin-ning Chu, note 135 above, at page 253; GOH Bee Chen, note 3 above, at page 42.

155   Wm Theodore de Barry, Wing-tsit Chan and Burton Watson (comp.), note 28 above, at page 169; Francis L.K. Hsu, note 4 above, at pages 315-316.

156   GOH Bee Chen, note 3 above, at pages 44-45; Chin-ning Chu, note 135 above, at page 253; V.R.Burkhardt, note 115 above, at page 77; Sarah Rossbach, note 135 above, at pages 121-122; Francis L.K. Hsu, note 4 above, at page 104.

157   V. R. Burkhardt, note 115 above, at page 219.

158   GOH Bee Chen, note 3 above, at page 51.

159   For example, my grandparents originated from the Province of Fukien and therefore my family observes and celebrates this day.

160   V.R. Burkhardt, note 115 above, at page 1.

161   V.R. Burkhardt, note 115 above, at page 7.

162   V.R. Burkhardt, note 115 above, at page 142.

163   WONG Choon San, note 44 above, at page 75.

164   V. R. Burkhardt, note 115 above, at page 8; Sarah Rossbach, note 135 above, at page 121.

165   V. R. Burkhardt, note 115 above, at page 16.

166   GOH Bee Chen, note 3 above, at pages 53-54.

167   WONG Choon San, note 44 above, at page 114.

168   Wm Theodore de Barry, Wing-tsit Chan and Burton Watson

(comp.), note 28 above, at page 5.

169   V. R. Burkhardt, note 115 above, at page 119.

170   V. R. Burkhardt, note 115 above, at pages 3 and 36.

171   WONG Choon San, note 44 above, at page 121.

172   GOH Bee Chen, note 3 above, at page 55.

173   V. R. Burkhardt, note 115 above, at page 36.

174   WONG Choon San, note 44 above, at apage 136; V. R. Burkhardt, note 115 above, at page 42.

175   V. R. Burkhardt, note 115 above, at page 129.

176   V. R. Burkhardt, note 115 above, at pages 42 and 129.

177   GOH Bee Chen, note 3 above, at page 56.

178   J. D. Vaughan, *Tha Manners and Customs of the Chinese of the Straits Settlements*, Oxford University Press, Kuala Lumpur, 1977, at page 48.

179   WONG Choon San, note 44 above, at pages 144-147.

180   V. R. Burkhardt, note 115 above, at page 121.

181   WONG Choon San, note 44 above, at page 148.

182   GOH Bee Chen, note 3 above, at page 58.

183   V.R. Burkhardt, note 115 above, at pages 62-63.

184   V.R. Burkhardt, note 115 above, at pages 4 , 62 and 66.

185   V.R. Burkhardt, note 115 above, at page 75.

186   V.R. Burkhardt, note 115 above, at page 65; GOH Bee Chen, note 3 above, at page 59.

187   GOH Bee Chen, note 3 above, at page 36.

188   Michael Harris Bond and Kwang-Kuo Hwang, "The Social Psychology of Chinese People" in Michael Harris Bond (ed.), *The Psychology of the Chinese People*, Oxford University Press, Hong Kong/Oxford/New York, 1986, at page 225.

189   GOH Bee Chen, note 3 above, at page 63.

190   V. R. Burkhardt, note 115 above, at page 135.

191   Rene David and John E. C. Brierley, note 108 above, at page 518.

192   Derk Bodde and Clarence Morris, note 31 above, at pages 5-6.

193   Stanley Lubman, note 114 above, at page 1291.

194   Phillip M. Chen, *Law and Justice: The Legal System in China 2400 B.C. to 1960 A.D.*, Dunellen Publishing Company, New York, 1973, at pages 14-15; Derk Bodde and Clarence Morris, note 31 above, at pages 4 and 43-44; Jerome Alan Cohen, note 105 above, at page 1207; Sybille van der Sprenkel, note 41 above, at page 29; Stanley Lubman, note 114 above, at page 1290; Rene David and

John E. C. Brierley, note 108 above, at pages 518-519.

195   Jerome Alan Cohen, note 105 above, at page 1207.

196   Stanley Lubman, note 114 above, at page 1291.

197   Sybille van der Sprenkel, note 41 above, at page 114.

198   Jerome Alan Cohen, note 105 above, at page 1207.

199   Comment made by the late Tan Sri LEE Siow Mong, a prominent Chinese Malaysian. See GOH Bee Chen, note 3 above, at page 153.

200   GOH Bee Chen, note 3 above, at page 127.

201   Rene David and John E. C. Brierley, note 108 above, at pages 522-523.

202   Stanley Lubman, note 114 abpve, at page 1289; Derk Bodde and Clarence Morris, note 31 above, at pages 5-6.

203   Jerome Alan Cohen, note 105 above, at page 1210.

204   Rene David and John E. C. Brierley, note 108 above, at page 520.

205   Phillip M. Chen, note 194 above, at pages 3-4.

206   Rene David and John E. C. Brierley, note 108 above, at page 520.

207   Rene David and John E. C. Brierley, note 108 above, at page 519.

208   This does not at all imply that the Chinese do not litigate at all, or that Westerners are invariably litigious. The point to be made here is that litigiousness is examined from the cultural perspective. Culturally speaking, the Chinese tend to shun litigation as a means of resolving disputes due to the various cultural norms and sanctions implicit in Chinese culture, for instance, the concept of face and the pursuit of social harmony. Westerners, on the other hand, who are more used to a confrontational style and adversarial system, are culturally more inclined towards litigation as a means of settling disputes. Of course, with an increasing awareness of the implicit ills of litigation such as high costs and inordinate delay, there is in recent times a movement away from litigation to mediation in settling disputes in Western societies.

209   S. Ting-Toomey, "Intercultural Conflict Styles: A Face-Negotiation Theory", paper presented at the meetings of the International Communications Association, New Orleans, May 1988, quoted in Harry C. Triandis, "Cross-Cultural Studies of Individualism and Collectivism", in John J. Berman (ed.), *Nebraska Symposium on Motivation* (1989) volume 37, at page 91.

210   Simon Roberts, *Order and Dispute: An Introduction to Legal Anthropology*, Penguin Books, Harmondsworth, 1979, at page 67.

211   Sybille van der Sprenkel, note 41 above, at page 117.

212   GOH Bee Chen, note 3 above, at page 159.

213   Sybille van der Sprenkel, note 41 above, at page 115.

214   Sybille van der Sprenkel, note 41 above, at pages 101 and 115; Stanley Lubman, note 114 above, at page 1298.

215   Sybille van der Sprenkel, note 41 above, at page 101.

216   Rene David and John E. C. Brierley, note 108 above, at page 519.

217   Francis L. K. Hsu, note 4 above, at page 381.

218   Francis L. K. Hsu, note 4 above, at page 151.

219   Rene David and John E. C. Brierley, note 108 above, at pages 523-524.

4 The Psychology Of Chinese Negotiation

Introduction

The aim of a negotiation is to reach an agreement by the parties concerned. The methods used, strategies adopted, styles displayed, and techniques employed depend to a large extent on the negotiators themselves and their inter-personal skills.[1] If the negotiators share a similar culture, the negotiation process could be skilful, strategic or tactical without culture being a stumbling block.[2] In contrast, if they do not share a similar culture, the cultural differences might impede an otherwise smooth negotiation.[3] In attempting to master effective negotiating skills or methods, one has to realize, too, that not only do different people negotiate differently, but different people from diverse cultural backgrounds possess particular perceptions of negotiation.[4] Thus, in a cross-cultural negotiation, one has to be constantly aware of the unconscious forces of the different cultural norms which may be present, and which may operate to undermine effective communication.[5]

Chinese-style negotiation may come across as puzzling or baffling to the Western negotiator who is used to his or her own customary ways and unaccustomed to the Chinese ways.[6] It is necessary to analyse the significant role assumed by the cultural dynamics in a Chinese negotiation.[7] It is useful to look at certain common and prominent cultural traits occurring in Chinese negotiation. It may be observed that the Chinese art of negotiation is founded predominantly upon their homocentricity. The majority of the cultural dynamics at play, therefore, represent manifestations of homocentrism, illustrating the Chinese principally relational manner of interacting with people and doing things.[8]

A complete study of the psychology of Chinese negotiation requires that one deal with certain social precepts, such as the ancient wisdom of Chinese geomancy, as well as some age-old taboos. These aspects are relevant in one's business dealings with the Chinese. Otherwise, one may be bewildered when, for no apparent reason, one's negotiation with the Chinese comes to a halt on account of what the Westerner is likely to dismiss as superstition. The Westerner is inclined to label as superstition any observation that bears no rational basis or that which cannot be scientifically proven by objective means, such as experiments. The Chinese, on the other hand, do not have such a problem. Subjective judgements, experiential guidance, wisdoms of the elderly, are some common factors shaping their beliefs. It is not at all essential that such beliefs must be tested for their truth by virtue of objective validators. In this sense, many a truth held by Chinese belief is prone to be dismissed as superstition by Westerners.

An appreciation of the Chinese cultural traits is helpful for one to become more aware and thus be a more effective and enlightened negotiator when negotiating cross-culturally with the Chinese.

The Psychology Of Negotiation

As a preliminary observation, it may be said that the Chinese are generally not comfortable with the idea of negotiation.[9] As a culture, the concept of negotiation is rather alien to them.[10] Theirs is a culture used to compromises and harmonizing of relationships. Implicit in the process of negotiation is the potential for conflict and confrontation. Generally speaking, the Chinese are culturally averse to confrontational behaviour.[11] The traditional Chinese emphasis based on the Confucian view of correct behaviour and conduct according to *li* [12] is on harmony in any inter-personal relationships.[13] The Confucian virtue of compromise is highly exalted by the Chinese.[14] In this connection, with regard to litigation, a Chinese proverb goes: 'Let householders avoid litigation; for once go to law and there is nothing but trouble'.[15] As such, confrontation is to be avoided at all costs.[16]

Additionally, for the Chinese, a people attuned to the idea of the cosmology of Heaven, Earth and Humanity, it may be said that: 'Balance is the great schema of the cosmos; Harmony is the universal path of life as a whole.'[17] The principle of harmony is seen to be of paramount concern. A negotiation which may possibly entail confrontation is therefore in contradistinction to the essential preservation of harmony.[18]

To this end, the Chinese can be said to be much like the Japanese who share, to a great extent, the Chinese traditionalist and Confucian heritage.[19] In fact, March might very well be referring to the Chinese in his following remarks:

> The Japanese instinct is for agreements worked out behind the scenes, on the basis of give and take, harmony and long term interest. In fact, except for a handful with extensive international experience, very few Japanese even know how to negotiate in the Western sense.[20]

The Western 'persuasive communicator'[21] skilled in a negotiation in which one party tries to gain advantages at the expense of the other also runs counter to the Chinese view of reciprocity of rights and mutuality of obligations ever present in a relationship. At this juncture, one recalls the Confucian five cardinal relationships in which the hierachical social structure embodies within it the reciprocal performance of duties and obligations. The principle of reciprocity to Chinese negotiators implies that everyone benefits in turn in an on-going business relationship. Thus, there is no hurry to exact one's pound of flesh.[22]

Another great contrast lies in the fact that Westerners are used to the idea of short-term benefits as opposed to the Chinese long-term vision.[23] This contrast bears direct consequences on the approaches to negotiations by these two culturally opposite groups, with the Chinese tending towards a relational style of negotiation while the approach of the Westerners tends to be transactional. Therefore, on the one hand, due to the Chinese desire to achieve and maintain long-term relations, trade-offs in a bargaining process are seen in light of reciprocity, not as weak negotiating. For example, a Chinese negotiator, in wanting to maintain long term business links, would be willing to accept reduced profits, a cultural trait shared by the Japanese.[24] To the Chinese, winning and losing is not as important as giving and taking, for, in the long term view, a party must 'win' sometimes and 'lose' at other times. The pragmatism of the Chinese is seen in the preservation of long-term good working relationships.[25]

In contrast, the emphasis of the Western party is not upon relationships but transactions.[26] The Western party thus desires an outcome in that particular transaction which yields a result most pleasing to him or her without worrying about long term links.[27]

This above apparent dichotomy between the Chinese and the Westerner may be attributable to the Chinese orientation towards homocentrism or collectivism as opposed to the Western inclination towards egocentrism or individualism.[28] As Triandis puts it, 'The point is that in a society where harmony is the ideal and 'doing the right thing' is essential for good relations, one often does what one believes to be socially desirable even if one's attitudes are inconsistent with the action.'[29] For the Chinese who perceive themselves as part of a larger whole, it becomes their natural tendency to behave in conformity with socio-cultural expectations which often involve a set of inter-personal obligations. Individual wants, therefore, come second to collective welfare, and mutuality becomes the guiding norm.[30]

While it is true that the Chinese largely believe in the relational ways of negotiating due to the fact that Confucianism has been a pervasive influence on the Chinese in business and commerce,[31] it should also be added that they subscribe to the philosophies of Sun Tzu whose brilliant military strategies have been found applicable in business dealings.[32] There is a popular Chinese maxim to the effect that 'the business world is likened to a battlefield'.[33] Chinese cultural traits such as patience and gathering information may be attributable to Sun Tzu's philosophies.[34]

Cultural Traits

What follows is an outline of the prominent cultural traits which one may encounter in one's negotiation with the Chinese. It is important to note that this represents an attempt at general observations regarding Chinese-style negotiation. The validity of these observations may vary in accordance with the negotiators, since negotiation itself is very much an inter-personal exercise, and much depends on the inter-personal dynamics involved.[35] The golden rule for negotiators is to always keep an open mind, and be ready to discard one's predictions as the occasion requires.

For instance, in cases in which the Chinese negotiators are Westernized, in the sense of having been Western-educated and being more adept at Western culture, they tend to feel less bound by traditional Chinese (Confucian) values.[36] Their style, then, may depart to a large extent from being influenced by Chinese cultural norms which might be alien to Chinese traditionalists, while their modern ways may come across as familiar to the Westerner.[37] Westerners negotiating with westernized Chinese will find the latter sharing some common bases, perhaps being more direct in communication and maintaining frequent eye contact, for example. This may lead one, then, to ask the question in relation to the Chinese negotiator: how does one know about his or her pre-disposition ? There is no quick or short answer to this question. One can only but try to find out the background of one's negotiating counterpart, either through one's contacts or personal experiences. Acquiring such information prior to a negotiation might go a long way towards minimizing blunders, and heightening one's negotiating skills through an awareness of the psyche of one's negotiating counterpart.[38]

Trust or Trustworthiness

Trust is a concept valued highly by the Chinese and also

represents to them a good working rule.[39] Its significance may be traceable to the Confucian insistence on being trustworthy in one's word when one is dealing with others.[40] For instance, *The Analects* provides: 'Make it your guiding principle to do your best for others and to be trustworthy in what you say'.[41] Hall and Ames point out that the concept of 'living up to one's word' is so major that it occurs 'some forty times in *The Analects*'.[42] In the Confucian tradition, living up to one's word is a major moral virtue.[43] The Confucian Chinese is trained from young to subscribe to the notion of 'My word is my bond.' It is regarded as a great dishonour for one not to live up to one's word, entailing the grave consequences of the loss of face.

For the Chinese, the principle of trust is fostered readily in the family environment. During early times, and nowadays to some extent, Chinese businesses have been family concerns.[44] As such, it is inconceivable that family members will betray one another for self-gain. On the contrary, it is perceived that family members will work together for the collective good. The principle of trust, therefore, has become rooted in practice in the family environment, and the Chinese seek to extend and familiarize it in their social and economic circumstances.[45] The meaning of trust, as pointed out by Redding and Wong,

> referred not only to credit, in the sense of goods or service lent without immediate return against the promise of a future repayment, or to 'credit rating', which is an assessment made by a lender of the risks involved in extending credit to a specific individual; it further carried the connotation of a person's total reputation for trustworthiness and in this sense was a statement of a person's social and psychological characteristics as well as strictly economic reliability.[46]

This does not mean that every Chinese negotiator is a trustworthy person and is above suspicion. What it essentially means is that the Chinese see no basis for entering into negotiations which are aimed at long term objectives and which go to provide mutually acceptable gains if, at least on a broad framework of how things are to operate, either party is constantly on guard and cannot leave better judgement to the other party in times of necessity. There should be scope for either party to act appropriately and contingently in aid of mutual benefits. However, this can only be achieved through some form of mutual reliance and, ultimately, on trust. Without trust, it is difficult to envisage how the business partners are going to operate on a long term basis.[47] To cite an example illustrating the importance of trust, Cohen relates a personal negotiating experience with the Chinese:

> I recall one 1979 negotiation in which the chief Chinese negotiator resisted our efforts to insert a provision in the contract by saying to his American counterpart: 'You know, Mr Blanton, we don't disagree with what you've just proposed, but we don't think it necessary to write it into the contract. After all, you and I trust each other, and we're going to be the ones who implement the contract. You know our tradition. We believe in a handshake. If the parties write a lot of details in a contract, Chinese think that means the parties don't trust each other. It is unattractive.[48]

Friendship

Implicit in the concept of trust is friendship.[49] The Confucian emphasis on the virtue of living up to one's word is premised upon the notion that it is 'the necessary condition for establishing the relationship of "friendship", and for winning the continuing support of the people'.[50] Breth and Jin observe that 'friendship and trust remain the cornerstone of successful Chinese-foreign business relations'.[51] The Chinese are, therefore, particular about establishing friendships or relationships before they enter into business dealings.[52] This may bear reference, too, to the Chinese cultural trait of being largely homocentric or collectivistic rather than being egocentric or individualistic.[53] The idea of business partners being friends brings not only material advantages, but social advantages as well. A Chinese proverb goes: 'When at home, you depend on your parents. When you leave home, you depend on your friends.' Friends are, therefore, people one calls on in times of need. With the Chinese, this cannot be more true.[54]

The principal element of trust which the Chinese seek cannot come about if there is no sign of friendship in a business relationship. As has been pointed out, 'Friendship and trust are two essential prerequisites for successful business negotiations and the Chinese are not prepared to undertake ventures with foreign companies and individuals if they do not display these important behavioural traits'.[55] This situation is more acute in the case in which the Western business partner is a complete stranger. 'This is because the Chinese place so much emphasis on friendship and trust when dealing with the foreigners.'[56] Although 'trust' in this sense is not absolute, it is a factor much treasured by the Chinese in that without trust, it is hard for them to discern as to whether or not business partners have long term mutual gains in mind. It is only when the Chinese believe that there is at least some trust present that they are likely to continue business dealings.

The discovery of mutual friends on either side is regarded as an important asset and facilitator in Chinese-style negotiation. The Chinese place trust in friends, and mutual friends of negotiating parties generate the much-needed overall trust.[57] For instance, a study done in Hong Kong has found that 'business contacts are friends, and virtually all business is based on personal contacts'.[58] It is, therefore, essential that when one is planning to do business with the Chinese, one begins by researching the possible connections or contacts of their Chinese counterparts. These connections and contacts act as an initial catalyst for trust to develop. The Chinese certainly feel more comfortable and at ease if they deal with people whom they can relate to, and not merely to talk with just to do business together. The Chinese also believe that if people regard each other as friends, no problem can appear too insurmountable. Friends are also more likely to perform favours when requested to do so.[59]

Because of the Chinese reliance on friendship, there is a high possibility of business dealings operating smoothly and without much open conflict. However, it must be stated that friendship in the context of Chinese commercial negotiation cannot be taken in the (Western) literal sense. '... The Chinese concept of friendship and more specifically their expectations of what friends should be willing to do for each other goes well beyond American notions of friendliness.'[60] Parties could be viewed as friends, even though the emotional bond between them may not be strong or substantial, as long as there is a tacit understanding that assistance will be rendered within one's means upon request.[61] In this way, the concept of friendship can operate in a most powerful way.[62] With the Chinese, there is present an almost compelling social sanction to act upon this notion of friendship. Otherwise, one's reputation is at stake and one could be punished by way of social ostracism, the heaviest penalty of all.[63]

This concept of friendship may contain many social tiers. For instance, if one's business friend is more senior in age to one, one has to accord due respect and one is expected to behave appropriately so as not to upset this hierachical structure.[64] This may also mean that one is expected to compromise a little more. A lack of understanding of such an inherent social hierachy would be detrimental to the Western negotiator who is more likely (culturally) to try to treat each one as his or her equal and thus inadvertently offend the Chinese party.

Gift-giving becomes relevant in the context of establishing and developing relationships or friendships. Gifts symbolise an earnestness to cultivate and maintain inter-personal goodwill.[65] The Westerner may look askance at the custom of gift-giving: 'in the West a gift that seems inappropriately lavish can have overtones of an ulterior motive, and in certain situations, might even be suspected of being in the nature of a bribe'.[66] What is important to realize is that despite any hidden intentions, it is the Chinese way of 'giving face' to the recipient, and thus initiating friendship and establishing rapport. One should also note that it is customary for the Chinese to thank the giver for the gift and then to put the gift aside. The Chinese consider it rude to open the present in front of the giver. Also, this goes to preserve the face of both parties, in case the gift, when unwrapped, turns out to be something inappropriate. Opening the gift later may save potential embarrassment for both sides.[67]

Partaking in meals serves a functional perspective in Chinese culture.[68] In observing customs, there are numerous occasions and festivities which invariably involve feasting. Feasting, to the Chinese, is not just an enjoyable activity; it is also the Chinese way of a constant fostering of relationships.[69] This is due to the congenial atmosphere a meal tends to create.[70] The Chinese are famous for sitting through lengthy meals.[71] During a meal, it is not an improper thing for one to discuss some aspects of business, particularly in pursuing the fine points which meet with deadlock at the formal negotiating table.[72] As Cohen validly observes:

> Many a problem can be solved more readily by negotiators who have established a close personal relationship than by those who keep their distance. Generally, it is desirable for negotiators to be frank with each other about perceived concerns and 'to open their hearts' as the Chinese say, rather than hold back inscrutably, and it is often easier for the Chinese to do this during informal contacts than in the regular meetings.[73]

In contrast, the Westerners distinguish between business and pleasure and tend to work through a meal to get things done.[74]

Bond and Hwang observe that the notion of friendship calls into play other Chinese cultural traits such as *mien-tze* (face), *guan-xi* (relationship or connection), *ren-ch'ing* (favours), and *pao* (reciprocation).[75] They are social expectations based on each. For instance, on the strength of one's relationship (*guan-xi*) with the other, one is expected to provide assistance and in this respect, may be called upon to grant favours (*ren-ch'ing*). 'Face' as a strong social mechanism will be dealt with in the succeeding section. With regard to *pao*, in a closely-linked social structure in which inter-dependence is not only desirable but inevitable, the Chinese generally believe in reciprocating favours.[76]

One can, therefore, appreciate that the idea of friendship or relationship is culturally desirous for the Chinese. This is due to the fact that achieving it would mean a smoother business venture, one premised on trust, long term gains, and dispute resolution.[77] As has been pointed out, 'Without doubt, the key to successful business dealings with the Chinese lies in the establishment and promotion of friendships. The Chinese will only negotiate seriously with foreign organizations and individuals that they are familiar with and whom they trust and respect.'[78]

However, one also has to recognise the fact that it is extremely time-consuming to try to establish a relationship.[79] Moreover, the Westerner, who is more transaction-oriented, is not one particularly interested in forming a relationship so long as the business deal can be struck. Be that as it may, there is no quick remedy.[80] If one is interested in doing business with the Chinese, one must be attuned to the Chinese desire for a long term relationship based on trust and harmony. Immediate short-term gains are less desirable to the Chinese than long term possibilities.[81] The point cannot be underscored enough that the Westerner has to learn to persevere: he or she has to sell himself first before he or she sells the goods.

Face

The Chinese have an obsession with the concept of face, which operates as a powerful social sanction. Kirkbride and Tang perceptively remark thus: 'The concept of face in social interactions is universal but is particularly important to the Chinese'.[82] As Pye puts it:

> The heavy use of shame as a social control mechanism from the time of early childhood tends to cause feeling of dependency and anxieties about self-esteem, which naturally produces self-consciousness about most social relationships. As a result, a great deal can be gained by helping the Chinese to win face and a great deal will be lost by any affront or slight, no matter how unintended.[83]

Being overly concerned with face-saving can also result in an over-sensitive nature. This could make the Chinese rather easily offended by unintentional remarks made by the Western counterpart. Sometimes statements made can be taken at their literal value thereby causing an erosion of confidence in a business relationship or unnecessary misunderstanding. It must be borne in mind that face-saving is not just the fear of self-embarrassment. It goes deeper than that. The Western party must try to be alert to this Chinese sensitivity in order not to cause offence unnecessarily.[84]

The concept of face is the Chinese equivalent of 'honour',[85] the value of which, as a social control mechanism, cannot be under-estimated. It constitutes a powerful factor in enforcing existing rules of behaviour by securing conformity to social norms. Van der Sprenkel refers to the principle of face as 'a constant concern to stand well in the opinions of others and in one's own opinion of oneself'[86] in order to ensure a smoother ordering of society. Face-saving, in the Chinese context, carries the dualistic aspects of self- and other-relatedness.

In the Chinese conception, in addition to *mien-tze* , face can also be interpreted as *lien*. When transliterated, both *mien-tze* and *lien* refer to the physical feature, i.e. face. However, they differ in their metaphorical connotations: *mien-tze* amounts to the 'prestige and reputation'[87] of a person, which could be increased or decreased, whereas *lien* means 'good character and personal integrity',[88] to be preserved intact or forfeited.[89] In securing obedience, *lien*   plays a more important role. The phrase, *pu yao lien,* meaning 'to forfeit face' is taken to be very serious breach of conduct. Hu points out that it is the fear of losing *lien* which 'keeps up consciousness of moral boundaries, maintains moral values, and expresses the force of social sanction'.[90] In this regard, therefore, it is the loss of *lien* which amounts to the loss of face that provides the social sanction. Kirkbride and Tang succinctly describe the precept of face in the following manner:

A person is socially condemned if he has no *lien* and is seen to be unsuccessful and low in status if he has no *mien-tze.* They are externally mediated and people interact with a purpose to add, give, take, compete, exchange or borrow 'face'.[91]

Bond and Hwang classify face into six categories:[92]
1.   Enhancing one's face: this is achieved by emphasizing one's abilities in accordance with prevailing social norms.
2.   Enhancing other's face: this can take the form of compliments, and a consideration for others.
3.   Losing one's face: bringing shame, or having shame brought, upon oneself as a consequence of socially inappropriate behaviour.
4.   Hurting other's face: causing another party to lose face through insensitive behaviour on one's part.
5.   Saving one's face: behaving in such a manner as to preserve one's pride.
6.   Saving other's face: behaving in such a manner as to preserve the pride of another party.

The Chinese are nearly always instinctively guided by the principle of face as a strong social precept.[93] In a negotiation, the Chinese think it rude to offend, for this will result in the other party losing face. It is important to preserve the face of the other party in order to maintain dignity and harmony.[94] Related to this concept of face is the need for the Chinese party to get to know his or her counterpart, a process which could take time, and during which the Chinese party could seem to be in agreement with his or her counterpart. To the Western negotiator who is culturally unaware of such a Chinese trait, it can be both misleading and frustrating because he or she may go away thinking that an agreement has been achieved, when in fact there is some distance to go before a final agreement is reached.[95]
    Another instance of face-saving behaviour is through subtlety.[96] Any attempt at a direct or blunt confrontation is viewed by the Chinese not only as an unfriendly act, but is regarded as gross misbehaviour and is strictly to be avoided. Bedi recalls the following incident concerning an Australian's insensitivity to the Chinese concept of face:

I know of an Australian manager who was admired back home for his blunt and forthright manner. Soon after his transfer to Hong Kong, he was involved in some price negotiations in China. He told a Chinese official in Ghuangzhou to his face that he was lying about the lower price of plastics from a competitive source. Two horrified Hong Kong Chinese employees who were present later told top management that one sentence had wiped out months of hard work.[97]

Due to the social stricture of the concept of face, the Chinese tend towards circuitous explanations at the risk of being misunderstood. Western observers, used to forthrightness and candidness, may accuse the Chinese of insincerity as such. However, on the contrary, the Chinese treat a display of courtesy, politeness and correct behaviour with due regard to face as sincerity.[98] One thus witnesses a clash of cultural norms. It is therefore essential to obtain the Chinese meaning of behaviour consistent with the dictates of face.

The preoccupation with the concept of face has its negative effects. One also has to bear in mind the Chinese long-term vision in their negotiations. Bound concurrently by the concept of face and long-term objectives, in a commercial negotiation, this may mean that they could have agreed to items they otherwise might not have agreed to but for the fact that they feel bound to carry through for fear of loss of face.[99] Additionally, a Chinese negotiator may be inclined to forsake some things in order to reap some future gain. Even if a deal may appear to be unfavourable, it still may be regarded as part of a larger bargain. In the meanwhile, by the act of preserving the face of the other, parties are enabled to gain trust and friendship.[100] However, as we have examined, such fear of loss of face is a real fear, and operates as a real sanction to secure compliance.

Guan-xi or Personal Relations

Closely tied to the concept of 'face' is the principle of *guan-xi*, meaning 'relationship' or 'connection'. 'It can be described as a special relationship individuals have with each other in which each can make unlimited demands on the other.'[101] As Smith puts it, 'The *guan-xi* system is as important as ever. What makes you important to someone else in a business relationship is not who you are, but whom you know'.[102] It was earlier stated that the Chinese generally believe in reciprocity of rights and mutuality of obligations. For the Chinese, culturally speaking, there is a great deal of inter-dependence on one another.[103] The whole social fabric revolves around this kind of mutual dependence. When a business partner becomes a friend in the eyes of the Chinese party, that partner is expected to render assistance whenever and wherever possible.[104]

This can oftentimes be viewed as rather onerous. This is because one may wonder when such obligations end. The fact of the matter is, they do not end.[105] It is not strictly *quid pro quo*. It may be said that one is under a continuous obligation for the rest of one's lifetime. The impact *guan-xi* has on a business negotiation is that it puts one in a vulnerable position, and may even have the effect of depriving one of negotiating power. This is because the power of *guan-xi* is so strong that one is expected to perform, or render assistance the other asks of one and it is almost impossible to refuse such requests for fear of making the other lose face thereby jeopardising one's relationship with the other.[106] In such a situation one is virtually left with no choice but to comply or conform.[107] Of course, it goes without saying that the same is expected of the other party.

Ren-ch'ing or Personal Goodwill

This may be likened to asking someone to perform favours.[108] In the Western sense, whether or not one agrees to perform a favour is dependent on one's convenience and voluntary agreement.[109] In the Chinese sense, it may entail an element of involuntariness, depending on the favour asked and the degree of the relationship that exists between the negotiators.[110] The closer the degree of relationship or friendship, the more one is expected to comply and feel duty-bound to carry out the request.[111] The sense of obligation is compelling.

Like *guan-xi, ren-ch'ing* is another attendant feature of friendship or relationship whereby the web of dependence is woven around the social bond or tie.[112]

Pao or Reciprocation

The quality of friendship enables the Chinese party to seek to iron out differences amicably (with a view to preserving long term relations), to make compromises, and to rely on assistance when called for, a quality linked to dependency, reciprocity or mutuality.[113] The Chinese understand fully well that there can be no taking without giving. And that it does not matter when or how many times one gives (provided the giving is within reasonable limits), for their actions are premised upon the notion that there is an eventual balance between retribution and reward. In a society which is structured hierachically, and where individuals perform according to one's and other's needs, there is certainly scope for reciprocation.[114]

For the Western negotiator, reciprocity or mutuality, though important, does not tend to rest on a long-term perspective.[115] As earlier stated, the Westerner is more interested in transactions occurring from time to time, not in long-term relations. As such, it is more difficult for them to abide by constant mutuality. He or she is dictated principally by short-term attainable goals.[116] Within this kind of time framework, the suggestion of ongoing mutuality runs opposite to his or her aims in a business deal.[117]

Patience

In Chinese philosophy, the quality of perseverance is highly valued.[118] It is a virtue that one should try hard to cultivate. To be patient is to be virtuous.[119] One, therefore, does not go about demanding things or favours. Rather, one performs good deeds, awaits recognition, and is accordingly rewarded. It is immaterial how long it may take for one's superior to recognise one's qualities before rewards are given. It is enough that one acts appropriately in the knowledge that the rewards will come one day.[120] Such faith enables the Chinese to cultivate extreme patience and to persevere.[121] One may assert that perseverance is an inherent Chinese quality, a quality which they are capable of displaying in any circumstance: social, economic, or political.

In economic circumstances, negotiating with the Chinese requires the utmost patience, for the Chinese can, to the Western observer, be unusually patient: '... the first rule in negotiating with the Chinese is the need for abiding patience.'[122] In the same vein, Breth and Jin state that 'one of the most frustrating aspects of doing business with China is the extraordinarily long time it takes to get things done. ... The Chinese have traditionally believed in doing things slowly and carefully.'[123] The Chinese commercial negotiator may tend to appear unhurried, calm, and under no pressure of deadlines.[124] The Western negotiating counterpart should try to avoid aggressive behaviour, abusive or offensive language, or show signs of annoyance, for 'the Chinese place considerable emphasis on poise, reason and self-control'.[125] In this regard, the Confucianist *Doctrine of the Mean* asks the individuals to exercise self-restraint in their behaviour. Assertive or aggressive behaviour is interpreted as being rude and offensive.[126] In this context, one is reminded of the association with the concept of face. Angry utterances in public such as at the negotiating table are likely to cause the Chinese negotiators to lose face, or to make them feel uncomfortable that the Western negotiators have caused their own loss of face as a result of their inability to exercise emotional self-control.[127]

Pye observes:

> The vast majority of our American informants said that a most difficult thing they had to learn about doing business with China was to disregard Chinese heroic rhetoric about catching up and to adopt the guiding principle of patience. They said repeatedly the ultimate secret of successful negotiations with the Chinese was to repress any urge to hurry the process along.[128]

Similarly, Sinclair and Wong remark that 'to do successful business in China you need large reservoirs of three personal attributes. The first is patience. The second is patience. The third is patience.'[129] In a recent study by Eiteman, patience has been found to be a strength for American executives dealing with Chinese joint-venturers.[130]

Patience in the context of a business relationship requires one to have the 'endurance and intellectual fortitude'[131] to cater to every possible factor that may arise in the business dealing.[132] Consequently, it demands thorough and unstinting preparation.[133]

Gathering Information

The Chinese have a particular affinity with gathering information before entering into any deal. March makes similar observations with regard to the Japanese.[134] He even comments that information gathering is so significant for the Japanese that it has become 'institutionalised'.[135] With regard to information gathering, Sun Tzu's axioms become highly relevant when applied to the field of commerce. These are axioms which point towards 'knowledge of one's own resources and capabilities, intelligence about the field of battle and the enemy's strength, patience, and whatever dissembling is necessary to deceive and catch the enemy off-guard'.[136] As will be explained in the succeeding Chapter, these axioms are not contrary to the Chinese cultural predisposition towards a relational approach, as the Chinese tend to hold the view that opposites are complementaries. Some of these axioms are stated below:

1.   'To defeat the enemy psychologically is the superior strategy. To defeat the enemy militarily is the inferior strategy.'[137]

- This axiom suggests that if one has sufficient information regarding one's opponent, one may then be able to defeat him or her.

2.   'The warrior's way is one of deception. The key to

success is to capitalize upon your power to do the unexpected, when appearing to be unprepared.'[138]

    - This relates to having information about what the opponent may expect and to use this knowledge to one's advantage.

    3.   'It is a doctrine of war not to assume the enemy will not come, but rather to rely on one's readiness to meet him; not to presume that he will not attack, but rather to make one's self invincible.'[139]

    - This refers to keeping oneself fully informed at all times in order to be prepared to meet all contigencies.

    4.   'Know the enemy, know yourself; your victory will never be endangered. Know the ground, know the weather; your victory will then be total.'[140]

    - This suggests that a thorough knowledge of the situation allows one to gain the final victory.

Information gathered could relate to the potential business partners themselves, the nature of the business involved, or other associated matters.[141] It is not uncommon for the Chinese to do thorough background research into all these preliminary essentials before they agree to meet with the new partner, or to begin undertaking business discussions.[142] This is not to say that the Western party regards information as unimportant. What is emphasized here is the degree and extent. The Western party must, of course, have been satisfied as to the soundness of the business venture before a willingness to do business. However, the Chinese party is often not satisfied with merely peripheral enquiries. A thorough investigation into all possible areas of the business deal must be done. This, again, can be very time-consuming and may easily frustrate the Western party who is more keen to close the deal as quickly as possible.[143]

Delay In Decision-Making

Even when to all appearances a deal has been struck, the next obstacle the Westerner is likely to face is an inordinate delay in decision-making by the Chinese party.[144] This is not unusual because the Chinese are very careful in ensuring that they know precisely what they have agreed to before deciding to commit themselves.[145] Due to their non-confrontational nature, it is abhorrent for them to raise issues or question certain aspects of the deal once concluded. With such propensity for harmony in a relationship, they are doubly careful that a decision once reached has been based on close scrutiny and wise deliberation.[146] This is another time-consuming exercise. At this juncture, fuelled by the desire to achieve the deal, the suspense can be a little too much to bear for the Westerner.[147]

Compromise

The Chinese value compromises.[148] They believe a great deal in give-and-take. It is important for them to be aware that their negotiating counterpart is equally capable of arriving at compromises rather than a strict insistence on rights. The ability to accept compromises reflects one's willingness to make sacrifices at times for the common good.[149] This, in turn, produces harmony in a relationship. Harmony is highly regarded by the Chinese who go to lengths to avoid upsetting any inter-personal imbalance.[150] For them, preserving friendship and long term relations is more crucial than immediate gains. This is based on a very practical philosophy that monetary gains once lost may be regained by some other means and at some other times, but the same is not the case with injuring friendships.[151]

To this end, the Western negotiating party must act flexibly and try to view compromises not in the light of losses but in that of retreating for the long-term good. Western culture is used to a win-lose situation based on the adversarial model[152] and it is sometimes difficult for the Westerner to view a given situation with a different set of cultural eye-glasses. The Chinese keenness to arrive at compromises represents one of their negotiating strengths in that they are always seeking 'win-win' results based on long-term objectives.[153]

Compromises are not always assessed in material terms.

In a business negotiation, one is likely to conceive of forgoing material or tangible advantages for the sake of the other party but ultimately for the true purpose of putting oneself in the good books of the other in the hope of concessions from the other party. The Western negotiator is trained to think in terms of concessions, not compromises. By concessions is meant that it is acceptable for one to concede a little, or to forgo what one can afford, with the consequence that the other party will do the same because one cannot be expected always to give.[154] Viewed in this light, concessions then serve the purpose of fulfilling one's negotiating goals or strategies. Such strategies may be seen as short-term measures. This, very clearly, runs counter to the Chinese long-term objectives.

Compromises, on the other hand, are not analysed in the same vein. Compromises involve one party meeting the other party half-way. In this way, it is akin to sharing the risks and burdens. This requires a great deal of mutuality, reciprocity and inter-dependence, made possible in light of long term relationships.[155] Culturally speaking, the Chinese are used to such ideals, based on homocentrism or collectivism, as opposed to Western individualism. In the latter conception, correct behaviour lies in how much one can obtain for oneself. With the Chinese, it is how much one can forgo for the sake of the greater common good.[156] As such, a Western negotiatior, when negotiating with the Chinese, must be able to identify the Chinese preferences for compromises rather than concessions, and to understand the rationale behind compromises.

Flexibility

In negotiating, the Chinese emphasize a great deal on flexibility. They do not believe in rigid terms and unchangeable conditions. As a matter of fact, their philosophic outlook emphasizes constant changes.[157] For instance, the Confucian teaching in *I Ching* (*The Book of Changes*) cautions humanity against adopting 'a fixed attitude which is forcefully maintained under any circumstances'.[158] Similarly, according to Sun Tzu, 'Of the five elements (metal, wood, water, fire and earth), none is always predominant; of the four seasons, none lasts forever; of the days, some are long and some are short, and the moon waxes and wanes'.[159] This philosophy suggests the impermanence of things.

It is little wonder, then, that in contractual matters, the Chinese prefer to agree on general principles and broad terms,[160] which could be accommodated in a 'Memorandum of Understanding' or a 'Document of Intent', documents which are not as rigourous as contracts but, nonetheless, still carry a binding sense of honour for the Chinese. Other details may be developed with time and amended in accordance with changes since the parties have already established their friendship and trust, possess long term objectives and have mutual benefits in mind.[161]

The Chinese attitude towards flexibility can be exasperating for the Western business partner for he or she is accustomed to firm agreements on every single detail.[162] However, the Chinese like to think that they are reasonable people. On such a basis, they feel that if a business outline is generally agreed upon, it is useless to attend to every detail with firmness, especially when the business risks are not too great, because circumstances may change. Parties should, therefore, try to negotiate on an ongoing basis in respect of the deal and not be hampered by rigidities.[163] Provided that the parties act reasonably, then there is nothing to which they cannot subsequently agree for the good of both. This flexible approach seems to the Chinese more sensible and equitable.[164]

A parallel situation can be found with the Japanese.[165] As March puts it: 'The fundamental Japanese approach to contracts is to emphasize the relationship being created, instead of the document being drawn up.'[166]

Flexibility among the Chinese may be misinterpreted by the uninitiated Western negotiator as a sign of changeability or fickle-mindedness. However, the Chinese see no wisdom in rigid adherence to apparently minor terms and conditions. It is not uncommon for one to come across the Chinese aversion to the Western insistence on written contracts.[167] In many cases where contracts have been entered into, it is not uncommon for these contracts to be filed away and treated as mere memoranda.[168] As mentioned earlier, the Chinese view written contracts as a lack of trust (and friendship) between the parties.[169] Also, contracts may be amended from time to time accordingly. Given that this is the case, the more sensible thing to do is to allow parties the flexibility to deal with contigencies as they arise, and to make compromises as the situations deem fit.[170] In this connection, a useful comparison may be made with the Japanese attitude towards contracts:

> Contracts are foreign to the Japanese ways of doing business... [T]he Japanese don't like contracts and tend to feel that if personal trust and integrity are absent the mere possession of a piece of paper will not salvage the situation... The Japanese prefer to place their trust in people rather than on paper.[171]

Viewed in the light of the Chinese emphasis on long-term relations, such flexibility seems to benefit both parties.[172] An agreement in broad principles, therefore, enables the parties to act flexibly with reference to all the details embodied in the agreement. These broad principles refer to the actual objectives of the business dealings themselves.[173]

Good Memory

Chinese education takes great pride in teaching and re-inforcing rote-learning as the primary learning method.[174] Chinese schools are famous for testing knowledge through how much one can commit information to memory, especially through rote-learning.[175] Such memory training may explain why the Chinese possess a good and tenacious memory.[176]

What transpires at meetings is often carefully stored away in the brain, to be resurrected when the occasion requires. Thus verbal promises made by a Chinese negotiator's counterpart can be quoted verbatim at a later date, and the counterpart held to his or her promises. This appears to be the case even though the

Chinese negotiators within an organization may have changed, for information is carefully passed on to the succeeding negotiator.[177] In this respect, the advice given is to 'master the record',[178] and to be careful about one's utterances.

Status

The Chinese are considered to be conscious of status.[179] The Confucian legacy of a set of social hierachical order implies that one always stands in a definite relationship with the other, in a superior or inferior position in accordance with appropriate circumstances.[180] For example, the father is regarded as the head of the family and is not to be contradicted.[181] However, in the father's work place, his employer is superior to him.

Ranking is therefore an important exercise in order for one to know how to behave accordingly in a given situation so as not to offend.[182] It also helps to explain why the exchange of business cards is important, as it immediately establishes the position of the respective parties, makes one become aware of each other's status and rank, and to address and deal with each other appropriately.[183] Business cards, in the Western context, are informative whilst in the Chinese context, serve a communicative purpose. Such subtle communication comes to light especially so since the Chinese are used to high-context communication. In addressing the Chinese party, one may find that he or she prefers to use the designated title such as President Lee, or Chairman Tan.[184]

Ambiguity

Cross-cultural communication may become difficult in instances where the uninitiated Western party meets with a Chinese 'Yes'. For fear of offending or embarrassing the Westerner, a Chinese may sometimes say 'Yes' when he or she actually means 'No' or 'Uncertain'.[185] It is then left to the Western counterpart to interpret the real meaning.[186] This can be extremely difficult. The

Chinese believe that it is impolite to reject another's request, or to turn someone or something down.[187] Due to this, a 'No' answer is often an impolite answer, or may offend.[188] As Bedi puts it,

> An anxious-looking pair of Western businessmen are sitting opposite their poker-faced Chinese counterparts over the negotiating table. The foreign boss whispers to his junior, 'Is is possible to ask if their "maybe" really means "maybe", or does it mean "no" or "probably no" or "possibly" or "definitely not" ?'[189]

A 'No' answer also causes the other person to lose face due to one's directly negative reply.[190] In another example, Cavusgil and Ghauri point out that "'maybe' and 'inconvenient' mean 'impossible' in Chinese and Japanese cultures".[191]

The Westerner may tend to interpret such Chinese behaviour as insincere. In fact, it has nothing to do with insincerity, but with cultural norms and expectations.[192]

As Mason observes:

> When engaged in business negotiations, as in other situations, a Chinese person may feel that a direct 'no' would be embarrassing to both parties, and try to convey his disagreement by more indirect methods, such as evading the question or remaining silent. The Western businessman should therefore be sensitive to this, and learn to interpret the signals which his Chinese counterpart is giving out.[193]

The Western negotiator should be aware of this Chinese culturally inherent practice so that he or she can understand better their inter-personal relationship and communication. The best guide in interpreting such ambiguities is to rely on one's intuition. Where possible, one could also approach an intermediary.

Task Versus Time Concept

In undertaking to do a project or an assignment, it is the habit of the Westerner to make payment based on the time it takes to complete it. For the Chinese, the payment is referable to the actual job itself.[194]

For instance, if one engages a landscaper to beautify one's garden, the Chinese will want to know how much is to be paid for the task. Time for completion is a separate matter for joint consideration. Conversely, the Westerner charges according to the time taken to finish the job, the most usual calculation being based on hourly rates. A non-Westernized Chinese is often uneasy with such hourly calculation, for he or she is more accustomed with payment according to the task completed. Hourly rate calculation could lead the Chinese party to suspect the other party of trying to cheat deliberately by prolonging the time it may otherwise take to complete the task.

This differing cultural orientation has to be appreciated in order to minimize any misunderstanding. Otherwise, each may be readily puzzled by the other party's customary behaviour.[195]

Non-Verbal Communication

Non-verbal communication occupies an important role in the effective understanding of another person's message.[196] It refers to 'the use of subtle signs, signals or cues in human interaction'.[197] It is, therefore, important for one to be aware of the cultural differences in the divergent interpretation of non-verbal signals, such as body movements or gestures.[198]

Nodding   Body language is yet another grey and complex area of cross-cultural communication. The Western party should not interpret a Chinese nod for a 'Yes'. Very often, such a nod may mean no more than that 'I hear what you are saying' without necessarily meaning that 'I agree with what you are saying'.[199]

Simply jumping to conclusions in the belief that a nod is the procurement of agreement can result in disastrous outcomes and cause misunderstandings.

Tone of Voice Due to the fact that the Chinese generally abhor confrontational or aggressive behaviour, it becomes natural to expect that they tend to prefer soft-spoken people. A low tone of voice is preferred in negotiations.[200]

Feet-Pointing The Chinese regard it as bad manners for one to point one's feet at one another, or for one to reveal the soles of one's feet to the person opposite one.[201] Such insensitivity and lack of respect may even amount to an insulting and offensive behaviour.[202]

Eye-Contact While Westerners regard eye-contact as essential in showing one's sincerity and earnestness, the Chinese consider a general lack of eye-contact as social courtesy. Talking to someone without looking straight into another's eyes is regarded as showing respect and politeness.[203]

Ancient Wisdom : *Feng Shui* Or Chinese Geomancy

On a discussion of *feng shui*, we once again recall the Chinese cosmology of Heaven, Earth and Humanity, and the intricacies that link them together. The guiding principle is harmony: harmony in aligning oneself with the natural order, and harmony in one's actions vis-a-vis one another.[204]

Feng shui may be traceable to the idea that because humanity is a product of the universe, one's house or burial place must be arranged in accordance with the harmony of natural forces, i.e. with wind and water.[205] *Feng Shui*, literally taken to mean 'wind' and 'water', 'is the art of adapting the residences of the living, and the resting places of the dead, so as to co-operate and harmonize with the local currents of the cosmic breath'.[206] The cosmic breath is considered the life force or energy on earth, which force or energy 'ripples water, creates mountains, breathes life into plants, trees, and humans, and propels man along a life course'.[207] Westerners refer to this form of Chinese divination as geomancy. However, as Rossbach points out, geomancy approximates the meaning assigned to *feng shui* but is not an exact translation.[208]

With regard to the origin of this belief and practice, Rossbach writes:

> For all the mystery that surrounds it, *feng shui* evolved from the simple observation that people are affected, for good or ill, by surroundings: the layout and orientation of workplaces and homes. In addition, the Chinese have long observed that some surroundings are better, luckier, or more blessed than others. Every hill, building, wall, window, and corner and the ways in which they face wind and water have an effect. They concluded that if you change surroundings, you can change your life. The aim of *feng shui*, then, is to change and harmonize the environment - cosmic currents known as *ch'i* - to improve fortunes.[209]

Feng shui may trace its beginnings to the Chinese discovery of rice cultivation at around 3,500 B.C. through the scientifically-based method of noting watercourses. Meandering and gently flowing rivers were found to suit the growth of crops better than did fast flowing ones. By adapting appropriately to their natural environment, the Chinese have been able to reap wealth from nature.[210]

Feng Shui is also basically a personal doctrine: what is ideal or favourable for one may have the opposite effect on the other.[211] This is due to the fact that one interacts in a personal fashion with the universe, for example, by contributing one's breath to it as well as drawing from it.[212] With such personal chemistry, there seems to be no universal application of *feng shui* rules. Notwithstanding this, some *feng shui* aspects affecting the environment have been popularised by the Chinese as common doctrines. For example, one should not locate one's house right at the end of a cul-de-sac, thus facing the entrance of the road, as it is believed that such a location may attract wandering spirits into one's home.[213]

The observance of *feng shui* is popular in the Asian

region and in Australia.[214] The Hongkong Bank of Australia situated in Sydney, for instance, recently consulted two *feng shui* masters after the Bank employees experienced a series of mishaps. According to a press report,

> Western businesses in Hong Kong have long accepted the importance of *feng shui* for their local employees and customers, while for Hong Kong Bank of Australia parent Hongkong and Shanghai Banking Corporation it is also part of the corporate culture.[215]

The relevance of one's realization of the Chinese belief in *feng shui* is to enable one to become an empathetic negotiator. In real estate matters, for instance, Australian real estate agents, when told of some basic *feng shui* rules, can improve their competency in advising their Chinese clients of suitable acquisitions.[216] Their knowledge and sensitivity to this ancient Chinese culture will not only impress their clients and achieve sales, but may operate to enhance their businesses as these clients spread the good word amongst their friends and relatives. I personally know of an Australian building consultant who lived for several years in Hong Kong and was, thus, conversant with the idea of *feng shui*. He has many Asian clients, and in fact, has dealt substantially with Singaporeans.[217]

In general business, too, the *feng shui* concept of harmony means correct timing is significant for businesses to prosper.[218] I am not referring to the general business person's idea of correct timing in business ventures. That, too, is important. But, in the Chinese sense, there is a deeper and more complex divination to decipher the proper time to commence a venture. For example, whilst in Malaysia, I once acted as a solicitor for a Hong Kong Chinese investor. The contract had already been agreed upon, and my client's counterpart who was of Indian origin was anxious to have a speedy execution of the contract. This could be attributed to the fact that business people are often afraid of a change of mind by either party given a time lapse. However, my client insisted that the signing of the contract could only take place the next day based on good *feng shui* to bless its beginning. Once explained to the Indian businessman, this attitude was fortunately shared and understood.

The idea of *feng shui* also goes to support the Chinese characteristic emphasis on relationships -- in this case, their relationship with nature for the betterment of humanity and their relating with nature in furtherance of human conditions. It is important to note that in the Chinese worldview, a harmonious human environment is linked with, and is a result of, a harmonious natural environment. Maintaining harmony is seen as essential in the preservation of relationships.[219]

Cultural Taboos

Burkhardt states that a taboo is 'a Polynesian term for a system, or act of setting apart a person, or thing, as accursed, or sacred.'[220] It includes anything considered by a society as something 'not done'. In this respect, the Chinese tend to have many cultural taboos. In such circumstances, their actions are dictated not by rational choices, but by fear of the supernatural. Too much belief in cultural taboos could affect their negotiation power because they cannot help their own actions or non-actions.[221] They then act out of a sense of self-preservation. The Western negotiator who becomes aware of some of these taboos will be better able to understand why there may be stumbling blocks in their negotiation.

There are various cultural taboos, ranging from the significant to the insignificant. Some of these common taboos appear below.

Numerology

The fascination with numerology is not the concern of the Chinese alone. Suffice it to say that the Chinese, firm believers of the notion of luck, have come to attach luck to some numbers and regard some others as signifying bad luck or disasters.[222] To the Chinese, numbers 9 and 1 are regarded as very auspicious for 9, being the largest number, connotes fullness, and 1 signifies the birth or the beginning.[223] In addition, 9 is homonymic with 'long life';[224] hence, its attraction for the Chinese who believe strongly in longevity.[225]

Certain numbers are considered impropitious by the Chinese and are to be avoided at all costs. The aversion to particular numbers can be a result either of a general cultural aversion or due to particular personal reasons. For instance, the number 4 is a number generally regarded by the Chinese as an impropitious number.[226] This is because '4' sounds like 'death' in Mandarin, Cantonese or Hokkien pronunciation.[227] The Chinese thus fear that this number may attract death, or some other calamity. In Hong Kong, Rossbach reports that 'Chinese buyers particularly shun number 424: 'die and die again'.[228]

One may question the relevance of such a taboo in a business negotiation. It can indeed be relevant. For instance, if a car seller tries to sell his or her car which has the number 4 on its number plate to a Chinese, he or she is unlikely to procure a sale. And, if a real estate agent is trying to sell a business or office complex and the street number of the complex is number 4, the potential Chinese buyer will probably be put off.[229] In this connection, it is interesting to note that the Brisbane City Council recently decided that new streets will not carry house numbers ending in 4.[230] Their decision is an expedient one, in view of the strong Asian migration and investment in Brisbane, and is seen as culturally responsive. Real estate agents were reported as saying that they had unsaleable homes because of the cultural aversion to this number.[231] Equally interesting has been the response of average ethnocentric Australians who have expressed their dissatisfaction over the Council's decision.[232]

In sharp contrast, the number 8 is highly desired by the Chinese as an auspicious number. 'Eight' is homophonic with 'prosperity' in Mandarin or Cantonese and is, therefore, much sought after by them.[233] For example, it is common to find cars with number plates like '888' belonging to Chinese owners.

Such a psychological attachment or aversion to numbers can play a significant role in a Chinese commercial negotiation in that the Chinese could be influenced in the decision-making process by these external factors. He or she may be guided, in the eyes of the Westerner, by superstition rather than rational choice.

However, if the Western negotiating counterpart is aware or made aware of such inclinations, their communication process might be less riddled with mystery, and less impeded by possible misunderstanding.

Colours

Generally speaking, colours arouse our imagination. Most people also tend to attach certain significance to colours.[234] For the Chinese, some colours have special meanings.[235] This is because they believe that 'one's destiny can be shaded by the colour of one's house, clothes, office, and so on'.[236] It is important for one to be aware of this factor so that one does not easily, though unintentionally, offend the Chinese by the wrong use of colours.[237]

For instance, white or black are considered colours one would wear during mourning.[238] To present white flowers to a Chinese host on auspicious occasions is to greatly offend, for white flowers signify death.[239]

On the other hand, the Chinese love red for it carries the meaning of happiness, prosperity, warmth and strength.[240] We noted earlier that during the observance of customs and celebration of festivities there is a popular use of the colour red. This is based on the belief that red not only brings good luck, but may increase one's wealth and fortune as well.[241]

Symbolism in Gifts

Symbolism plays a meaningful part in gifts.[242] The Chinese go to lengths to select gifts which symbolise 'long life, affluence, happiness, and posterity'.[243] Chinese words are monosyllabic and sounds vary in four tones.[244] Hence, homophones are quite common. For this reason, when choosing a gift, one has to try to get an item which is not homophonic with another word denoting negativity. An example is a clock as a birthday gift. This is because 'clock' is homophonic with 'termination'.[245]

Therefore, one should never present a clock as a gift to a Chinese on his or her birthday, as it is tantamount to wishing death upon the recipient.

A vase is homophonic with 'peace', and is a welcome gift to a home owner as a bringer of peace and tranquility.[246]

During Chinese New Year festivities, mandarins are extremely popular gifts for they connote sweetness. Mandarins, too, are very brightly coloured and are, therefore, deemed to convey the message of happiness and prosperity.[247]

Gifts are often well-intentioned gestures, and givers are desirous of plenty of goodwill. It is indeed unfortunate if, through ignorance or inadvertance, one's gift produces the opposite result by causing hurt or offence. Such complexities can appear to be rather daunting to the uninitiated but one should, in the spirit of human understanding, endeavour to build bridges and close gaps by cultivating cross-cultural awareness.

Conclusion

In human interaction, our natural desire is to seek agreement and to avoid unnecessary conflict. Cross-cultural interaction has its inherent pitfalls due to one's possible lack of knowledge or perception of the other party's different ways of doing things. The homocentric Chinese can appear to be an enigma to the average Westerner whose values and behavioural rules are principally guided by a different set of norms. As a consequence, misunderstandings may easily arise.

The impact of culture on the Chinese in their business behaviour has been a subject of study.[248] Cultural influences, shaped in the main by Confucianism and flavoured by Sun Tzu's philosophies, have operated to make the Chinese negotiating styles, strategies and negotiation process vastly different from Western ways. With increased global and transnational business activities, cross-cultural negotiating (and in this context, Sino-Western negotiating) necessitates an understanding and appreciation of not only how culture predominates, but how it functions and influences. Otherwise, to the uninitiated, behaviour perceived as strange can be both baffling and exasperating.[249]

In order that a negotiation process have a fruitful outcome, it would be expedient for a Western party to note, and attempt to cultivate, some of the Chinese positive traits in negotiation. For instance, the rule on patience.[250] The Chinese regard the lack of self-control in one's emotions and language not only highly undesirable, but very rude and offensive and disharmonious. They shun abusive language and aggressive behaviour. The Westerner should try to be aware of this and learn to exercise self-restraint. To the Chinese, it very often enhances a relationship if the Westerner attempts not only at understanding some aspects of Chinese culture, but practises what he or she has learnt. In a negotiation process, achieving a wavelength in which both parties operate from similar vantage points should help them arrive at acceptable agreements much more quickly.

An understanding of the ancient wisdom of *feng shui* and cultural taboos by the Westerner can help to strengthen Sino-Western communication. An ability to create goodwill far outweighs any unintended offence. The knowledge that a number, a colour, or a gift may offend will prepare one culturally in extending one's goodwill not only consciously, but effectively and meaningfully.

In analysing the psychology of Chinese negotiation, one has to bear in mind the Chinese orientation towards homocentrism, the dominant feature of which is the primacy of people, not things. To disregard this orientation, which calls for establishing and maintaining good human relationships, is to put a spanner in the works. On the other hand, eagerness for inter-personal goodwill and harmony puts the Westerner in a very strong position.

The central tenets of trust and friendship in Chinese negotiation are crucial to the Chinese relational approach to negotiation, as contrasted with the Western approach. The competitive spirit tends to prevail in a Western egocentric culture, with the result that the Westerners seem to exhibit a transactional style of negotiation.[251] Further, the Chinese relational style reinforces their long term objectives whereas the Western transactional style serves their short term goals.[252] With the latter, it is only where there is some degree of permanence in a relationship that the approach may become more co-operative.[253]

NOTES

1   On the insights of effective negotiation, see, for instance, Roger Fisher and William Ury, *Getting to Yes: Negotiating Agreement Without Giving In*, Penguin Books, New York, 1981; Herb Cohen, *You can Negotiate Anything*, Lyle Stuart Inc., Secaucus (New Jersey), 1980; and Gerard Nierenberg, *The Complete Negotiator*, Nierenberg & Zeif Publishers, New York, 1986.

2   See Robert Lawrence Kuhn, *Dealmaker: All the Negotiating Skills and Secrets You Need*, John Wiley & Sons, New York, 1988; Collin Rose, *Negotiate and Win*, SPA Books, Stevenage, 1989; Bill Scott, *The Skills of Negotiating*, Gower, Aldershot (Britain), Reprint 1989.

3   Donald Hendon and Rebecca Angeles Hendon, *World-Class Negotiating: Dealmaking in the Global Marketplace*, John Wiley & Sons, Inc., New York et al, 1990, at pages 49-50; S. Tamer Cavusgil and Pervez N. Ghauri, *Doing Business in Developing Countries: Entry and Negotiation Strategies*, Routledge, London and New York, 1990, at page 111; Jeffrey Z. Rubin and Frank E.A. Sander, 'Culture, Negotiation, and the Eye of the Beholder' (1991) *Negotiation Journal* at pages 249-254.

4   GOH Bee Chen, 'Understanding Chinese Negotiation' (1993) *Australian Dispute Resolution Journal*, at page 178; Guy Olivier Faure, 'Negotiating in the Orient: Encounters in the Peshawar Bazaar, Pakistan' (1991) *Negotiation Journal* at pages 279-290; S. Tamer Cavusgil and Pervez N. Ghauri, note 3 above, at pages 82-83.

5   See, for example, Edward T. Hall and Mildred Reed Hall, *Hidden Differences: Doing Business with the Japanese*, Anchor Press/Doubleday, Garden City, New York, 1987; and Don R. McCreary, *Japanese-U.S. Business Negotiations: A Cross-Cultural Study*, Praeger, New York et al, 1986.

6   Ray Stone, 'The Chinese Negotiating Game' (1988) 9 *The Practising Manager (Australia)*, at page 27.

7   The Japanese style of negotiation is said to be culturally

influenced: see Robert J. Walters, "'Now that I Ate the Sushi, Do We Have a Deal ?' - The Lawyer as Negotiator in Japanese-U.S. Business Transactions" [1991] 12 Northwestern Journal of International Law & Business 335, at page 341.

8   Paul S. Kirkbride and Sara F. Y. Tang, 'Negotiation: Lessons From Behind the Bamboo Curtain' (1990) 16 *Journal of General Management* 1, at page 6.

9   The Japanese share a similar tendency: see Robert M. March, *The Japanese Negotiator: Subtlety And Strategy Beyond Western Logic*, Kodansha International, Tokyo and New York, 1988, at page 15.

10   Robert M. March, note 9 above, at page 15.

11   Paul S. Kirkbride and Sara F. Y. Tang, note 8 above, at pages 6-7.

12   See Confucius, *The Analects*, (Translated with an Introduction by D. C. Lau), Penguin Books, London, 1979. For a detailed discussion of *li*, see Chu T'ung-tsu, *Law And Society In Traditional China*, Mouton & Co., Paris/La Haye, 1961, at pages 230-241.

13   Michael Harris Bond and Kwang-Kuo Hwang, 'The Social Psychology of Chinese People' in Michael Harris Bond (ed), *The Psychology of the Chinese People*, Oxford University Press, Hong Kong, 1986, at pages 214-216.

14   See Eric Lee, *Commercial Disputes Settlement In China*, Lloyds of London Press, London, 1985, at pages 1-4.

15   Stanley Lubman, 'Mao and Mediation: Politics and Dispute Resolution in Communist China' (1967) 55 *California Law Review*, at page 1296.

16   Michael Harris Bond and Kwang-Kuo Hwang, note 13 above, at pages 261-264; Paul S. Kirkbride and Sara F. Y. Tang, note 8 above, at pages 6-7. The fact that the Japanese are equally averse to the idea of confrontation can be seen in Robert M. March, note 9 above, at pages 84-85.

17   Adapted from *Chuang Tzu*, quoted in Michael Harris Bond and Kwang-Kuo Hwang, note 13 above, at page 213.

18   Paul S. Kirkbride and Sara F. Y. Tang, note 8 above, at page 6.

19   See Ryusaka Tsunoda, Wm Theodore de Bary and Donald Keene (compl.), *Sources of Japanese Tradition*, Columbia University Press, New York, 1958; Mark A. Zimmerman, *Dealing With The Japanese*, Unwin Paperbacks, London, 1985, at page 21; Chin-ning Chu, *The Asian Mind Game: Unlocking the Hidden Agenda of the Asian Business Culture - A Westerner's Survival Manual*, Rawson

	Associates, New York, 1991, at pages 181-183.
20	Robert M. March, note 9 above, at page 15.
21	Robert M. March, note 9 above, at page 15.
22	Harry C. Triandis, 'Cross-Cultural Studies of Individualism and Collectivitism' in John J. Berman (ed.), (1989) 37 *Nebraska Symposium on Motivation*, at page 60.
23	Robert O. Joy, 'Cultural And Procedural Differences That Influence Business Strategies And Operations in the People's Republic of China' in (1989) 54 *Advanced Management Journal* 29, at page 31.
24	Edward T. Hall, *The Dance of Life: The Other Dimension of Time*, Anchor Press/Doubleday, New York et al, 1984, at page 105.
25	Note the Chinese proverb: 'Friendship first, competition second'. See Michael Harris Bond and Kwang-Kuo Hwang, note 13 above, at page 263.
26	Jacques Rojot, *Negotiation: From Theory To Practice*, MacMillan, Hong Kong, 1991, at page 33.
27	Robert O. Joy, note 23 above, at page 31.
28	Michael Harris Bond and Kwang-Kuo Hwang, note 13 above, at pages 220-222, 227-229; Kuo-Shu Yang, "Chinese Personality And Its Change" in Michael Harris Bond (ed), note 13 above, at pages 147-148; Gordon Redding and Gilbert Y. Y. Wong, 'The Psychology of Chinese Organizational Behaviour' in Michael Harris Bond (ed), note 13 above, at page 285; Robert O. Joy, note 23 above, at page 30; Christopher J. Smith, *CHINA: People and Places in the Land of One Billion*, Westview Press, Boulder, 1991, at page 36.
29	Harry C. Triandis, note 22 above, at page 80.
30	Christopher Smith, note 28 above, at pages 34-36; Michael Harris Bond and Kwang-Kuo Hwang, note 23 above, at pages 254-258.
31	Carsun Chang, *The Development of Neo-Confucian Thought*, College and University Press, New Haven, 1957, at page 15. On the influence of Confucian ideology among the overseas Chinese, see Gordon Redding and Gilbert Y.Y. Wong, note 28 above, at pages 271-272.
32	Thomas Cleary (trans.), *Sun Tzu: The Art of War*, Shambhala, Boston & London, 1988; Samuel B. Griffith (trans.), *Sun Tzu: The Art of War*, Oxford University Press, London, 1963; M.W. Luke Chan and CHEN Bingfu, *Sunzi on the Art of War and its General*

Application to Business, Fudan University Press, Shanghai, 1989.

33   Quoted in Chin-ning Chu, note 19 above, at page 12.

34   Sun Tzu believed in a calculated and strategic approach to war as an inevitable human endeavour. His philosophies have been transplanted to the sphere of commerce and his Thirteen Chapters have been assimilated to be part and parcel of the traditional Chinese ways of doing business.

35   Chin-ning Chu, note 19 above, at page 7; Paul S. Kirkbride and Sara F. Y. Tang, note 8 above, at page 9.

36   Kuo-Shu Yang, 'Chinese Personality and its Change' in Michael Harris Bond (ed.), note 13 above, at pages 160-162 ; Hari Bedi, *Understanding the Asian Manager: Working with the Movers of the Pacific Century*, Allen & Unwin, Sydney, 1991, at pages 13-16.

37   Kuo-Shu Yang, note 36 above, at page 162.

38   GOH Bee Chen, note 4 above, at page 179.

39   GOH Bee Chen, note 4 above, at page 179; Ron Breth and Jin Kaiping, 'Negotiating the Contract' in *A Business Guide to China*, Victoria College Press, Burwood (Victoria), 1988, at page 163.

40   See *The Analects*, I: 5; I: 7; I: 13; VIII: 16; IX: 25; XII: 10. See also Chin-ning Chu, note 19 above, at page 244.

41   *The Analects*, I: 8, IX: 25, and XII: 10.

42   David Hall and Roger Ames, *Thinking Through Confucius*, State University of New York Press, Albany, 1987, at page 60.

43   David Hall and Roger Ames, note 42 above, at pages 56, 60-61.

44   Gordon Redding and Gilbert Y. Y. Wong, note 28 above, at page 281.

45   Gordon Redding and Gilbert Y. Y. Wong, note 28 above, at page 280.

46   Gordon Redding and Gilbert Y. Y. Wong, note 28 above, at page 281: the observation made was in connection with these authors' study of Chinese businessmen in Vietnam.

47   GOH Bee Chen, note 4 above, at page 180.

48   Jerome Alan Cohen, *Contract Laws of the People's Republic of China*, Longman, Hong Kong, 1988, at page 23.

49   The Chinese notion of friendship should be distinguished from the Western sense, otherwise a Western reader is likely to perceive it as no different and misunderstanding may ensue. In the Chinese sense, friendship is laden with obligations, with

expectations of what one party may be called upon to do for another, and a refusal to comply with another's requests seen as causing the other party to lose face and therefore as being highly undesirable. Establishing friendships or relationships, no matter how superficial or ritualistic as viewed from the Western perspective, is a necessary part of Confucian *li*, which, in the narrow sense, is linked to social etiquette or propriety. *Li* cannot be analysed to mean relationship per se. It is a social precept which varies in meaning depending upon the context used. However, the underlying observance of *li* is the establishment, maintenance and preservation of relationships in Chinese society, particularly hierachical relationships. It can, therefore, be appreciated that the Chinese sense of friendship is far more complex and culturally influenced than the Western perception of friendship. The Western approach is more rights-based, as opposed to the Chinese one of obligations-based. By this is meant that even when Western parties are good friends, they are at liberty to reject favours asked of them if they feel inconvenienced, unwilling or unable to perform the favours asked. Similarly, Westeners feel comfortable to exhibit confrontational behaviour with one another at the negotiating table or in public and yet afterwards socialize with one another without carrying the emotional baggage. In this connection, William Gudykunst states that people in individualistic cultures 'can argue over task-oriented issues and remain friends' whereas people from collectivistic cultures find it 'difficult to have open disagreement without one or both parties losing face': William Gudykunst, *Bridging Differences: Effective Intergroup Communication*, Sage Publications, Newbury Park (California)/London/New Delhi, 1994 (Second Edition), at page 197.

50 David Hall and Roger Ames, note 42 above, at page 61.

51 Ron Breth and Jin Kaiping, note 39 above, at page 172.

52 Lucian Pye, *Chinese Negotiating Style: Commercial Approaches and Cultural Principles*, Quorum Books, New York et al, 1992, at page 37. Pye adds that the same theme of friendship occurs with dealings with the Chinese in Hong Kong, Taiwan and Singapore.

53 See Gordon Redding and Gilbert Y. Y. Wong, note 28 above, at pages 283-285. Note the importance of family in Confucian ideology: see Christopher Smith, note 28 above, at page 35.

54 Lucian Pye, note 52 above, at pages 101-102.

55 Ron Breth and Jin Kaiping, note 39 above, at page 163.

56   Ron Breth and Jin Kaiping, note 39 above, at page 165.

57   Gordon Redding and Gilbert Y. Y. Wong, note 28 above, at page 281.

58   Gordon Redding and Gilbert Y. Y. Wong, note 28 above, at page 281.

59   Lucian Pye, note 52 above, at pages 89 and 107.

60   Lucian Pye, note 52 above, at page 23; see also pages 52, 100-103.

61   Lucian Pye, note 52 above, at pages 101, 107.

62   See Kevin Sinclair and Iris Po-yee Wong, *Culture Shock ! - China*, Graphic Arts Center Publishing Company, Portland (Oregon), 1990, Reprint 1993, at page 143.

63   See Gordon Redding and Gilbert Y.Y. Wong, note 28 above, at page 281; Sybille van der Sprenkel, *Legal Institutions in Manchu China: A Sociological Analysis*, University of London the Athlone Press, London, 1972, at page 31.

64   The Confucian tradition emphasizes the Five Cardinal Relations: sovereign-subject, father-son, elder brother-younger brother, husband-wife, and friend-friend. These relations are seen in a hierachical order, with the senior being accorded respect and privileges. See Michael Harris Bond and Kwang-Kuo Hwang, note 13 above, at page 215; Christoper Smith, note 28 above, at pages 34-35.

65   Chin-ning Chu, note 19 above, at page 252; Michael Harris Bond and Kwang-Kuo Hwang, note 13 above, at page 225; Ron Breth and Jin Kaiping, note 39 above, at page 166; Caroline Mason, *Simple Etiquette in China*, Paul Norbury Publications, Folkestone (United Kingdom), 1989, at page 31.

66   Mark A. Zimmerman, note 19 above, at page 70.

67   Caroline Mason, note 65 above, at page 18.

68   Michael Harris Bond and Kwang-Kuo Hwang, note 13 above, at page 225; Ron Breth and Jin Kaiping, note 19 above, at page 166; Jerome Alan Cohen, note 48 above, at page 25.

69   Caroline Mason, note 65 above, at page 33; Sybille van der Sprenkel, note 63 above, at page 115.

70   Ron Breth and Jin Kaiping, note 39 above, at page 166.

71   Jerome Alan Cohen, note 48 above, at page 25.

72   Ron Breth and Jin Kaiping, note 39 above, at page 166.

73   Jerome Alan Cohen, note 48 above, at page 25.

74   Jerome Alan Cohen, note 48 above, at page 25; Ron Breth and Jin Kaiping, note 39 above, at page 166.

75   Michael Harris Bond and Kwang-Kuo Hwang, note 13 above, at pages 223-226.

76   Lucian Pye, note 52 above, at page 37.

77   Ron Breth and Jin Kaiping, note 39 above, at page 167.

78   Ron Breth and Jin Kaiping, note 39 above, at page 171.

79   Ron Breth and Jin Kaiping, note 39 above, at page 163.

80   Chin-ning Chu, note 19 above, at page 243.

81   Ron Breth and Jin Kaiping, note 39 above, at page 171.

82   Paul S. Kirkbride and Sara F. Y. Tang, note 8 above, at page 7.

83   Lucian Pye, note 52 above, at page 101; see also Fanny M. C. Cheung, 'Psychopathology Among Chinese People' in Michael Harris Bond (ed.), note 13 above, at pages 205-207.

84   S. Tamer Cavusgil and Pervez N. Ghauri, note 3 above, at page 123.

85   Kenneth Scott Latourette, *THE CHINESE: Their History and Culture*, MacMillan Company, New York, 1964, at page 584.

86   Sybille van der Sprenkel, note 63 above, at page 99.

87   Sybille van der Sprenkel, note 63 above, at page 99.

88   Sybille van der Sprenkel, note 63 above, at page 99.

89   Paul S. Kirkbride and Sara F.Y. Tang, note 8 above, at page 7.

90   Hu Hsien-Chin, quoted in Sybille van der Sprenkel, note 63 above, at page 100.

91   Paul S. Kirkbride and Sara F. Y. Tang, note 8 above, at page 8.

92   Michael Harris Bond and Kwang-Kuo Hwang, note 13 above, at pages 246-248.

93   Lucian Pye, note 52 above, at page 101.

94   Paul S. Kirkbride and Sara F.Y. Tang, note 8 above, at page 8.

95   Paul S. Kirkbride and Sara F.Y. Tang, note 8 above, at page 8.

96   Ron Breth and Jin Kaiping, note 39 above, at page 165; Jerome Alan Cohen, note 48 above, at page 23.

97   Hari Bedi, note 36 above, at page 134.

98   Lucian Pye, note 52 above, at page 101.

99   Paul S. Kirkbride and Sara F.Y. Tang, note 8 above, at page 8.

100   Preston M. Torbert, 'Contract Law in the People's Republic of China' in Michael J. Moser (ed), *Foreign Trade, Investment and the Law in the People's Republic of China*, Oxford University Press, New York, 1987, at page 335.

101   Lucian Pye, note 52 above, at page 101.

102   Christopher Smith, note 28 above, at page 48.

103	David k. Eiteman, 'American Executives' Perceptions of Negotiating Joint Ventures with the People's Republic of China: Lessons Learned' (1990) *Columbia Journal of World Business* 59, at pages 64-65.
104	Lucian Pye, note 52 above, at page 101.
105	Lucian Pye, note 52 above, at page 107.
106	Lucian Pye, note 52 above, at pages 100-103.
107	Lucian Pye, note 52 above, at pages 101-103.
108	Michael Harris Bond and Kwang-Kuo Hwang, note 13 above, at pages 224-225.
109	Michael Harris Bond and Kwang-Kuo Hwang, note 13 above, at page 245.
110	Chin-ning Chu, note 19 above, at pages 237-238.
111	Chin-ning Chu, note 19 above, at pages 237-238.
112	Michael Harris Bond and Kwang-Kuo Hwang, note 13 above, at pages 224-226.
113	Lucian Pye, note 52 above, at pages 101-102.
114	Michael Harris Bond and Kwang-Kuo Hwang, note 13 above, at page 224.
115	Lucian Pye, note 52 above, at page 108.
116	Robert O. Joy, note 23 above, at page 31.
117	Robert O. Joy, note 23 above, at page 32.
118	Plum blossoms, the national flower of the People's Republic of China, have been selected for their persevering quality in winter (symbolic of one's perseverance in adversity).
119	*The Analects*, XIV: 30.
120	Confucius said: "It is not the failure of others to appreciate your abilities that should trouble you, but rather your own lack of them" in *The Analects*, XIV: 30.
121	Chin-ning Chu, note 19 above, at page 189.
122	Lucian Pye, *Chinese Commercial Negotiating Style*, oelgeschlager, Gunn & Hain, Publishers, Inc., Cambridge, Massacchusetts, 1982, at page 12; see also S. Tamer Cavusgil and Pervez N. Ghauri, note 3 above, at page 121.
123	Ron Breth and Jin Kaiping, note 39 above, at page 52, see also page 165.
124	The Japanese share the same trait: see Mark A. Zimmerman, note 19 above, at pages 64-65; Robert M. March, note 9 above, at pages 17-18.

125   Ron Breth and Jin Kaiping, note 39 above, at page 165; see Caroline Mason, note 65 above, at page 9.

126   Paul S. Kirkbride and Sara F. Y. Tang, note 8 above, at page 8.

127   This concept of face is more intricate and complex for the average Westerner to really grasp its full meaning. Suffice it to say that losing face operates as such a strong social sanction that amicable behaviour is always preferred to aggressive behaviour. However, this is not to say that one cannot find Chinese negotiators who are openly critical of others in public. The question is one of dominant tendency. For a useful comparison with the Japanese, see Mark Zimmerman, note 19 above, at pages 65-66.

128   Lucian Pye, note 122 above, at page 13.

129   Kevin Sinclair and Iris Wong Po-yee, note 62 above, at page 121.

130   David K. Eiteman, note 103 above, at pages 60-61.

131   Mark A. Zimmerman, note 19 above, at page 64.

132   S. Tamer Cavusgil and Pervez N. Ghauri, note 3 above, at page 121. In Sun Tzu's words, "keep him under a strain and wear him down" in *The Art of War*, I, 24.

133   Mark A. Zimmerman, note 19 above, at pages 64-65.

134   Robert M. March, note 9 above, at pages 29-31.

135   Robert M. March, note 9 above, at page 30.

136   Robert M. March, note 9 above, at page 30.

137   *The Art of War*, III: 3.

138   *The Art of War*, I: 17 and VII: 12.

139   *The Art of War*, VIII: 16.

140   *The Art of War*, III: 31; X: 26.

141   *The Art of War*, Chapter X.

142   GOH Bee Chen, note 4 above, at pages 185-186.

143   On a comparison with the Japanese, see Robert J. Walters, note 7 above, at page 338.

144   Ron Breth and Jin Kaiping, note 39 above, at pages 168-169; David K. Eiteman, note 103 above, at page 63.

145   S. Tamer Cavusgil and Pervez N. Ghauri, note 3 above, at page 121.

146   Lucian Pye, note 122 above, at page 106.

147   See Kevin Sinclair and Iris Po-yee Wong, note 62 above, at page 142.

148   Chinese culture is based predominantly on the Confucian virtue of

compromise. See Eric Lee, note 14 above, at pages 1-4.

149   In this connection, it is important to note the Chinese tendency towards collectivism in social governance.

150   Michael Harris Bond and Kwang-Kuo Hwang, note 13 above, at page 262.

151   Confucius said: 'If one is guided by profit in one's actions, one will incur much ill will' in *The Analects*, IV: 12 and in IV: 16: 'The gentleman understands what is moral. The small man understands what is profitable.'

152   Edward T. Hall and Mildred Reed Hall, note 5 above, at page 117. In contrast with Chinese collectivism, the Western worldview is premised on individualism.

153   GOH Bee Chen, note 4 above, at page 186; Preston M. Torbert, note 100 above, at page 335. For a similar approach with the Japanese, see Edward T. Hall and Mildred Reed Hall, note 5 above, at page 117: 'In Japan everybody must win.'

154   Ray Stone, note 6 above, at page 29.

155   Preston M. Torbert, note 100 above, at page 335.

156   Harry C. Triandis, note 22 above, at page 83.

157   Fung Yu-Lan (edited by Derk Bodde), *A Short History of Chinese Philosophy*, MacMillan Company, New York, 1948, at pages 19-20; Richard Wilhelm (translated by Irene Eber), *Lectures on the I Ching : Constancy and Change*, Princeton University Press, Princeton, 1979, at page 4.

158   Richard Wilhelm, note 157 above, at page 4.

159   *The Art of War*, VI: 31.

160   Robert O. Joy, note 23 above, at page 31; Julian Weiss, *The Asian Century: The Economic Ascent of the Pacific Rim - and What it Means for the West*, Facts on File, New York/Oxford, 1989, at page 84.

161   Lucian Pye, note 122 above, at pages 24, 32, and 109. A parallel tendency exists amongst the Japanese, see Robert March, note 9 above, at page 86; Robert J. Walters, note 7 above, at page 346.

162   Edward T. Hall, note 25 above, at page 104; Edward T. Hall and Mildred Reed Hall, note 5 above, at pages 128-129.

163   Chin-ning Chu, note 19 above, at page 239.

164   See Confucius, 'The gentleman is devoted to principle but not inflexible in small matters': *The Analects*, XV: 37.

165   Edward T. Hall and Mildred Reed Hall, note 5 above, at pages 128-129.

166   Robert M. March, note 9 above, at page 111.

167   In the Confucian view, one ought to be trustworthy in one's word: *The Analects*, I, 5, 7, 8, 13; IX, 25; XII, 10.

168   Chin-ning Chu, note 19 above, at page 239.

169   Jerome Alan Cohen, note 48 above, at page 23.

170   Chin-ning Chu, note 19 above, at page 239.

171   Mark A. Zimmerman, note 19 above, at pages 91-92. See also Edward T. Hall and Mildred Reed Hall, note 5 above, at pages 128-129.

172   Preston M. Torbet, note 100 above, at page 335.

173   Lucian Pye, note 52 above, at pages 51 and 109.

174   Learning by heart has been an enduringly traditional form of learning since the olden days: see Arthur Cotterell, *China: A Concise Cultural History*, John Murray, London, 1988, at page 193.

175   Francis L.K. Hsu, *Americans and Chinese: Passage to Differences*, The University Press of Hawaii, Honolulu, 1953, 1981 (third edition), at page 94.

176   GOH Bee Chen, note 4 above, at page 187.

177   Lucian Pye, note 52 above, at page 109.

178   Lucian Pye, note 52 above, at page 109.

179   Caroline Mason, note 65 above, at pages 28-30.

180   Lucian Pye, note 52 above, at page 102.

181   TU Wei-Ming, *Centrality and Commonality: An Essay on Confucian Religiousness*, State University of New York Press, Albany, 1989, at page 105.

182   Robert O. Joy, note 23 above, at page 30; see quotation by Hu Hsien-Chin (1948) at page 53 found in Sybille van der Sprenkel, note 63 above, at page 31.

183   Chin-ning Chu, note 19 above, at page 248.

184   Caroline Mason, note 65 above, at page 20. In this connection, Lee and Tan are surnames which, in the case of the Chinese, are placed before their given names.

185   Caroline Mason, note 65 above, at page 30.

186   Chin-ning Chu, note 19 above, at page 241; Hari Bedi, note 36 above, at page 149.

187   Robert O. Joy, note 23 above, at page 30.

188   Robert O. Joy, note 23 above, at page 30.

189   Hari Bedi, note 36 above, at page 149.

190   Robert O. Joy, note 23 above, at pages 30-31.

191   S. Tamer Cavusgil and Pervez N. Ghauri, note 3 above, at page 125.

192   Lucian Pye, note 52 above, at page 101.

193   Caroline Mason, note 65 above, at page 30.

194   Robert O. Joy, note 23 above, at page 31.

195   Robert O. Joy, note 23 above, at page 31.

196   R. Huseman , M. Galvin and D. Prescott, *Business Communication: Strategies and Skills*, Holt, Rinehart & Winston, Sydney, 1988 (third edition), at pages 225-230.

197   S. Tamer Cavusgil and Pervez N. Ghauri, note 3 above, at page 117.

198   Donald Hendon and Rebecca Angeles Hendon, note 3 above, at page 85.

199   The subtlety of head nodding is also discussed in R. Huseman, M. Galvin and D. Prescott, note 196 above, at page 228.

200   Robert O. Joy, note 23 above, at page 30.

201   Donald Hendon and Rebecca Angeles Hendon, note 3 above, at page 92; Robert O. Joy, note 23 above, at page 30.

202   For a similarity with the Thais, see S. Tamer Cavusgil and Pervez N. Ghauri, note 3 above, at page 124.

203   Robert O. Joy, note 23 above, at page 30; see also S. Tamer Cavusgil and Pervez N. Ghauri, note 3 above, at page 119.

204   Sarah Rossbach, *Feng shui: Ancient Chinese Wisdom on Arranging a Harmonious Living Environment*, Century, London at al, 1984, at pages 8-11.

205   Fung Yu-Lan, note 157 above, at page 130; Sarah Rossbach, note 204 above, at page 18.

206   V. R. Burkhardt, *Chinese Creeds and Customs*, South China Morning Post Publications, 1982, at page 111.

207   Sarah Rossbach, note 204 above, at pages 4-5 and 21.

208   Sarah Rossbach, note 204 above, at page 3.

209   Sarah Rossbach, note 204 above, at page 2.

210   Sarah Rossbach, note 204 above, at page 48.

211   V. R. Burkhardt, note 206 above, at page 114.

212   Sarah Rossbach, note 204 above, at page 21; Renee Weber, *Dialogues With Scientists and Sages: The Search for Unity*, Routledge and Kegan Paul, London and New York, 1986, at page 60.

213   A common Chinese belief.

214   Sarah Rossbach, note 204 above, at page 13; V.R. Burkhardt, note 206 above, at page 113.

215   The Australian Financial Review, 28 January 1994 .

216   Multicultural Times, 1 June 1994.

217   Mr Allan Manton of Dominion Homes on the Gold Coast, Australia.

218   Sarah Rossbach, note 204 above, at page 155.

219   John M. Koller, *Oriental Philosophies*, Charles Scribner's Sons, New York, 1970, 1985 (second edition), at page 3.

220   V. R. Burkhardt, note 206 above, at page 114.

221   See, for example, the Chinese refraining from purchasing houses with number '4' as reported in The Sunday Mail, 22 May 1994.

222   Sarah Rossbach, note 204 above, at pages 153-154.

223   Sarah Rossbach, note 204 above, at page 154.

224   Sarah Rossbach, note 204 above, at page 154.

225   V. R. Burkhardt, note 206 above, at pages 207-209.

226   The Sunday Mail, 22 May 1994.

227   Sarah Rossbach, note 204 above, at page 154.

228   Sarah Rossbach, note 204 above, at page 154.

229   Sarah Rossbach, note 204 above, at page 154.

230   The Sunday Mail, 22 May 1994.

231   One real estate agent quoted worked with Ray White in Brisbane.

232   The Sunday Mail, 29 May 1994 , at page 19 and 5 June 1994, at page 94.

233   Multicultural Times, 1 June 1994.

234   Sarah Rossbach, note 204 above, at page 121.

235   Sarah Rossbach, note 204 above, at pages 121-122; Chin-ning Chu, note 19 above, at page 163.

236   Sarah Rossbach, note 204 above, at page 121.

237   Sarah Rossbach, note 204 above, at pages 121-122; Chin-ning Chu, note 19 above, at page 163.

238   Chin-ning Chu, note 19 above, at page 163; Sarah Rossbach, note 204 above, at pages 121-122.

239   Donald Hendon and Rebecca Angeles Hendon, note 3 above, at pages 61-62 and 115.

240   Sarah Rossbach, note 204 above, at page 121; Chin-ning Chu, note 19 above, at page 163.

241   Sarah Rossbach, note 204 above, at page 121.

242   V. R. Burkhardt, note 206 above, at pages 205-206.

243   V. R. Burkhardt, note 206 above, at page 205.

244   Caroline Mason, note 65 above, at page 43.

245   Caroline Mason, note 65 above, at page 18.

246   V. R. Birkhardt, note 206 above, at page 206.

247   A popular custom among the Chinese.

248   See Gordon Redding and Gilbert Y. Y. Wong, note 28 above, at page 269.

249   Ron Breth and Jin Kaiping, note 39 above, at page 163.

250   David K. Eiteman, note 103 above, at pages 60-61.

251   In the Western world, a relational approach towards negotiation is now highly encouraged: see Fisher and Brown, *Getting Together: Building Relationships that Get to Yes*, Houghton Mifflin, Boston, 1988; William Gudykunst, note 49 above, at pages 207-221.

252   David K. Eiteman, note 103 above, at page 65.

253   See Jacques Rojot, note 26 above, at pages 32-33.

5 The Art Of War At The Round Table

Introduction

It is important for a Westerner entering a negotiation process with a Chinese party to note that the Chinese language is metaphoric, and it is very common for metaphors to be used in everyday conversations. What is perhaps surprising, from the Western perspective, is the extensive use of metaphors containing militaristic strategies which are applicable in normal life situations. The power of such metaphors lies in the employment of vivid images and production of effective messages. The closest Western equivalent is in the use of idioms and phrases. For instance, telling someone to 'make hay while the sun shines' comes across as far more effective than laboriously explaining to someone how to make full use of opportunities. Similarly, the Chinese are generally accustomed to a collection of idiomatic expressions which comprise normal, everyday and ordinary social utterances, so commonsensical in their usage that one could say that for the Chinese, what in the Western world constitutes formalised strategic thinking is nothing more than instinctive thinking. To cite a personal example, whenever I need to attend to some matter, my parents will often say: 'watch the situation and act accordingly'. This phrase, in fact, originates from one of Sun Tzu's famous militaristic principles, cautioning one to be always prepared, and to be flexible. I have often taken Chinese idiomatic expressions for granted, as natural as breathing. It was not until after my being exposed to Western education that I had the occasion to reflect upon Chinese and Western thinking processes.

Western education and training has always emphasized a logical and analytical approach to knowledge.[1] Chinese strategic negotiation as exemplified by the following exposition of the Thirty-Six Strategies may confound those trained in such an education. This is because elements in the Strategies could be interpreted, by a process of Western logical thinking, as being completely contradictory to my assertions in the previous chapters that the Chinese tend to profess a relational style, value friendships and harmony, and promote trust. Logical thinking is functionally exclusionary: things dissimilar are construed as polar opposites, or viewed as paradoxes. Such dissimilarities cannot, at one and the same time, accommodate or include each other on analysis.[2]

By way of contrast, the Chinese mindset operates very differently. Chinese education has always emphasized synthesis and an integrative approach to learning. Chinese thought patterns are essentially circular, as opposed to the Western linear form of thinking. In the Chinese mindset, different or dissimilar things are complementary opposites forming a unity, facets of a continuum. Such dissimilarities do not exclude one another; instead, they include one another when viewed as the ultimate unified whole.[3] In this way, the Chinese style of thinking virtually defies Western logic. From the Chinese perspective, a relational style of negotiating is not in conflict with strategic negotiation. A fundamentally Western appreciation will see them as conflicting concepts, requiring some harmonization or reconciliation.

Chinese strategic negotiation is an art as ancient as, and chiefly derived from, Sun Tzu's *Art of War*,[4] which is considered to be 'the most prestigious and influential book of strategy in the world today'.[5] According to Chu,

> The Chinese are a strategy-oriented people. Situations that, in Western minds, are handled by intuition or common sense are the subject of formalised strategies in Chinese thought. Even young children learn strategies for dealing with a wide variety of everday problems.[6]

The Thirty-Six Strategies have been transmitted from generation to generation amongst the Chinese by the most known, common and effective method: folklore.[7] It is said that

Chinese children -- particularly those who have received an education in Mandarin, have been made aware of them since childhood.[8] This is in order that as they enter adulthood, they will be able to recognise and so prevent certain Strategies being used against them, and conversely, to learn how to apply these Strategies when the circumstances so require.[9]

As a little child growing up in the rural part of Malaysia, I learnt the phrase: 'Of The Thirty-Six Strategies, the best Strategy is in running away'; and rather spontaneously, whenever there was perceived danger as we played children's games, I would utter this phrase and flee. This phrase, in fact, represents The Thirty-Sixth Strategy, the last of all the Strategies.[10] This Strategy finds its equivalent in the West in the following proverb: 'A person who runs away lives to fight another day'.

My young mind then had unwittingly absorbed an ancient part of Chinese culture without my truly appreciating the origin of the phrase, nor what all the Thirty-Six Strategies were about. What happened to me was not at all unique. Chu shares a similar sentiment: 'Being immersed in Asian culture, one absorbs strategic thinking unconsciously and learns to love the mental thrust-and-parry as a natural part of human interaction'.[11]

The compilation of *The Thirty-Six Strategies* in fact originates from ancient Chinese *bing fa*, meaning the rules of the warrior, or more commonly referred to as the art of war.[12] In this connection, it is important to note that the Chinese generally do not have a divisive view regarding what is military knowledge and what is civilian knowledge.[13] All knowledge is regarded as inter-related and applies equally well in all situations with suitable modifications.[14] This accounts for the popular usage of Sun Tzu's *The Art of War* in corporate management practices in modern day philosophy.[15] Additionally, as the maxim goes: 'the business world is likened to a battlefield'.[16]

The philosophic origin of *The Thirty-Six Strategies* is said to be the *I Ching (The Book of Changes)*.[17] 'Using the *I Ching*'s fundamental principle of ever-changing *Yin* and *Yang*, *The 36 Strategies* describes the methods for manipulating specific manifestations of the universal duality to one's advantage'.[18] In ancient Chinese philosophy, 'Yin' refers to the feminine or the negative and 'Yang' the masculine or the positive, the opposing forces which make up the duality of our existence.[19] The central teaching of *The Thirty-Six Strategies* is to focus on the present: the reality of the situation.[20] All reality comprises the opposing forces of positivity and negativity, of good and bad, of fortune and calamity, of success and failure. One should learn to be able to balance these opposing forces and achieve victory through reconciling these forces.[21] In a negotiation, for instance, whether or not one is able to fulfil one's objectives depends on how one views the reality of one's situation and how one achieves success despite one's interests conflicting with one's opponent's interests. Also, it is important to realize that one's reality changes with time, and to learn to perceive those changes.[22] When one is fully aware of one's reality in a given situation, one should know how to be flexible and respond appropriately, accordingly and strategically. Thus, success is not a consequence of divine intervention, nor a matter of miracles or luck. Success comes from grasping reality and the opportune application of the relevant strategy.[23]

The Thirty-Six Strategies appear as idiomatic expressions which are precise, concise and succinct. The majority of them, as we shall see, are worded dramatically. They are designed to deal with all manner of situations.[24] The key feature of these Strategies seems to be craftiness. One may seek to be artful or tactical depending upon one's given situation. The underlying principle is to attack the opponents' weaknesses, and avoid their strengths. Again, it needs to be stressed that this does not contradict relationalism, given the Chinese belief in the synergy associated with opposite ends. The skilled Chinese negotiators may use one Strategy at a time, or blend a variety of these Strategies to suit their needs in order to enable them to achieve their objectives.

What appears below is an exposition of The Thirty-Six Strategies which may be used at one time or another by Chinese negotiators. To the untrained or uninitiated Westerner, Chinese strategic negotiation can be dreadfully incomprehensible, vacillating between madness and magic. Some Westerners may consider the Chinese methods 'confusing, unprofessional and seemingly inappropriate'[25], but these criticisms are reflections of Western culture, whose values and those of the Orient part ways.[26] As Chu puts it, 'ethical distinctions are cultural'.[27] In strategic negotiation, both the Chinese and Western cultures have developed their respective and distinctive strategies, and both cultures possess their own validators for the practice of such strategies. In extreme situations, both cultures have also developed similar strategies which resemble crafty or even deceitful tactics which are often employed by the desperate negotiators to achieve their goals. For instance, the use of feminine charm to entice and soften a tough negotiator is a tactic which has been practised by both cultures since early times.[28]

It is not my intention to evaluate the morality or otherwise of the employment of any of The Thirty-Six Strategies. Rather, my task is based on an intellectual pursuit, aimed at a cultural exposition of the age-old Chinese strategies for the advancement of cross-cultural understanding in Sino-Western negotiating situations.

What now follows represents an outline of The Thirty-Six Strategies and their applications in the negotiating environment.[29] Due to the paucity of materials written in English, I have endeavoured to translate sources from Mandarin texts. In this exposition, I shall not be dealing with the historical context or successful usage of these Strategies in ancient times. I shall undertake a broad survey of The Thirty-Six Strategies and interpret their application in modern day negotiating situations.

The Thirty-Six Strategies

1.   *Crossing the Ocean Without the Sky Being Aware of it*

As human beings, we become suspicious when all around us, things appear to be hidden and locked away and intensely guarded. On the other hand, we tend to lose our watchful nature when everything is apparent and obvious, and we are in a victorious position. Such open display tends not to raise any suspicion in one and in fact, one may even go so far as to dismiss its insignificance.[30] It is precisely when one is not suspicious that one can be overcome by one's opponents.

As Chu postulates, 'To accomplish one's objective, it is sometimes necessary that a falsehood be openly displayed and the truth hidden. An opponent's attention is thereby focussed on the false situation, allowing the true objective to be accomplished easily without detection'.[31] She goes on to say that 'if we see a situation as a usual event, it arouses no suspicion. The darkest of secrets are often hidden in the open. *Yin* exists in *Yang, Yang* exists in *Yin*; light in darkness, darkness in light'.[32]

For instance, you might be anticipating a salary raise, only for your employer to tell you that the company is undergoing financial difficulties and may have to retrench some staff. The end result is that you are so happy to get to keep your job that you lose your passion about a raise. Your employer may in fact be employing this Strategy.

This Strategy therefore teaches us to be careful, to beware, and learn to see the obvious as not so obvious, and to be watchful for hidden intentions.

Conversely, it also teaches us that in order to win, being open artfully is more effective than using secretive ways. Open strategies can often distract a negotiator's attention and may cause him or her to concentrate on the unintended, thereby omitting the real objectives of the strategies.

2.   *Rescue the State of Chao By Surrounding the State of Wei*

When a negotiator is faced with a hopeless situation (metaphorically, the State of Chao), tackling the strong opponent headlong can be counter-productive and can cause further losses. In order to win, therefore, one should distract the opponent by diluting his or her resources (metaphorically, surrounding the State of Wei), utilising one's strengths against the opponent's weaknesses, and avoiding direct confrontation.[33]

This Strategy enables the negotiator to capitalize on his or her strengths and to use his or her strengths to overcome the opponent's weaknesses. It warns of the danger of trying to attack the opponent's strong points and suffering more losses as a result of one's already weak position.

As an example, if your opponents have an established overseas market for a product similar to yours, your venture into the same overseas market may be an uphill struggle, if not futile. However, it could be the case that by concentrating on the overseas market, your opponents may have neglected their own domestic market. Your competition in their domestic market may be more favourable. In time, your opponents may regard you as a formidable competitor and dilute their resources to cope with both their overseas and domestic markets. When this happens, you may be in a stronger position to compete with them in that overseas market as well.

3. *Use Another's Knife to Kill Someone Else*

This is a famous and common negotiating strategy. It connotes two senses. Firstly, it means using someone else's resources to advance one's position. Secondly, it means achieving a dual purpose: one manages to conserve one's resources and yet at the same time achieves one's goals through the defeat of the opponent by somebody else who may potentially be another opponent. The latter sense is considered a military high point.[34]

For example, in Australia, with regard to the first sense of this Strategy, the popular expression 'use other people's money' to enable one to accumulate wealth is a facet of this Strategy.[35] By borrowing from the bank to make acquisitions, one keeps one's savings and uses other depositors' money to enhance one's wealth. In this regard, this Strategy allows the negotiator to plan financially and make a purchase by using another's resources.

As another example of how this Strategy works, it may be the case that one's negotiating partner who represents the opponent may be a difficult person to deal with. One may be instrumental in the removal of one's negotiating counterpart by a subtle, manipulative and effective complaint by one to his or her superior or ally. By removing this person through manipulating somebody else to get rid of him or her, one may then proceed with fresh negotiations with a new person.

4.   *Make Your Opponent Work While You Rest and Reap the Rewards*

This Strategy teaches us always to be early, take charge and to be in control of the position.[36] By gaining and staying in control, the opponent has to work extra hard to keep up. This will result in the opponent exhausting himself or herself in a negotiation, particularly a protracted one, and eventually giving in to one's demands.[37]

Chu cites the following example of foreigners negotiating in China:

> When a foreigner has to live in Beijing for an indefinite period, he is at a distinct disadvantage in comparison to his Chinese counterparts. He is under a great deal of pressure, both financial and psychological, to strike a deal, any deal, in order to get back home in a timely fashion. For the foreigner, Beijing is one of the most expensive cities in the world. He must also cope with foreign food and a culture that is completely different from his own. Eventually, the strength of his negotiating position will be eroded and the Chinese position correspondingly strengthened.[38]

5.   *Loot While the Place is on Fire*

The best opportunity to strike presents itself when one's opponent undergoes an internal chaotic state. Chaos causes uncertainty and confusion and the opponent becomes most vulnerable to attack.[39] This Strategy aims at profiting from another's misjudgement or misfortune.

Thus, in a negotiation, one must seize opportunities as they come. As the proverb goes 'strike while the iron is hot'.

Negotiation is about getting a good bargain. Buying goods at company liquidation sales is a good example of this Strategy. Such sellers are undergoing hard times and want to clear their goods cheaply and quickly: bargain hunters are like looters attacking the vulnerability of the sellers.

6.   *Distract Your Opponent's Attention Eastward When You Mean to Attack Westward*

This Strategy ensures victory by capitalizing on the opponent's misjudgement or miscalculation as a result of the negotiator's use of distracting tactics. By diverting the opponent's focus elsewhere, one may cause him or her to commit an error of judgement. One then creates the opportunity to succeed in a negotiation virtually by default.[40]

However, the success of this Strategy lies in one's accurate prediction of the opponent's response. If one under-estimates the reaction of the opponent, or causes him or her to be suspicious of one's intention, this Strategy will then not produce the intended result.[41]

In an employment situation, it is common for a valued employee to disclose to the employer potential offers elsewhere. By doing so, the employer may bow to the employee's demands in an attempt to keep him or her.

7.   *Create Something From Nothing*

Chu states: 'The objective of this Strategy is to make the unreal seem real; the empty, full. If there is no wind, there are no waves. Wind must be created if waves are desired'.[42]

It is sometimes human nature to tend to act on hearsay, without checking or investigating the truth of the matter. Therefore, by spreading a rumour, one can confuse one's opponent into making an error of judgement, causing him or her to act to his or her detriment.[43] Hasty action by the opponent may bring benefits to one.

For instance, in the Autralian real estate industry, there are frequent media reports on possible rising interest rates for home loans, the prediction of peaking house prices, the 'don't miss out' advertisements, which are calculated to induce consumers into action and commit themselves to home purchases. Creating something from nothing clouds the decision-making processes of potential home owners who are pressurized into action for fear that the prophecies may come to pass.

8.   *Use the Secret Chern Chang Passage*

This Strategy, akin to the Sixth Strategy above, reinforces the value of preparedness.

By being prepared at all times, it becomes difficult for one's opponent to wait for an opportune time in order to strike. One should, however, attack when and where the opponent least expects it (metaphorically, using the secret Chern Chang Passage, a passage in China). One should appear to be weak when one is, in fact, strong, thereby causing the opponent to lose preparedness by his or her false arrogance.[44]

By deceiving the opponent as to the truth of the situation, one may secure victory through the element of surprise.

At a negotiation, for instance, if you are not getting through to the current party because of a weaker position which you occupy, you should, without this party's knowledge, secretly engage in negotiations with a new party. Your efforts with this new party may yield better results, and together you may defeat the former opponent, and catch him or her completely by surprise.

9.   *Watch the Fire Burning From the Opposite Riverbank*

Whenever an opponent suffers from internal chaos and conflict, one should be observant and assess the situation. Sometimes, the best thing to do is to do nothing while waiting for events to take their proper course and perhaps turn in one's favour.[45]

'A good strategist understands the best time for action and inaction.'[46] Similarly, a good negotiator cultivates a patient and observant attitude, then strikes when the opportunity is right.

It is also possible that the opponent's internal chaos is generated by one's other opponents. By doing nothing and observing the course of events, one may stand to gain as the two parties tire themselves through exhaustion of energy and depletion of resources.[47]

In the negotiation context, if your market competitors are locked in a conflict situation, the best thing to do is to act with indifference for the time being, while keeping abreast with the development of events. The engagement in the conflict will exhaust the energies and resources of your competitors. You should act only when the time is right, i.e. when events turn in your favour. Patience, and a good sense of judgement are essential.

10.   *Hide a Knife Behind a Smiling Face*

This Strategy attempts to deceive the opponent by one's insincere friendliness. One's goodwill may cause the opponent to repose trust and confidence in one. One then betrays this trust to achieve one's ends.[48]

Chu thus warns: 'Beware of smiling faces and effusive displays of friendship at the negotiation table'.[49]

The display of insincerity by one's negotiating counterpart for the purpose of achieving his or her own ends is a well-known and common psychological ploy. In business and commerce, just because others act with excessive goodwill to you does not indicate that they have your best interests at heart. The converse may be more true. You should, therefore, be always on guard, and be prepared for betrayal. This Strategy essentially reminds each one of us of the capriciousness of human nature.

11.   *The Plum Tree Sacrifices for the Sake of the Peach Tree*

The plum tree and the peach tree are metaphoric: the former refers to something small and insignificant, and the latter means something big and important.[50] This Strategy teaches the value of making appropriate sacrifice. In any negotiation, one must learn to give up something in order to gain something else. It is desirable that one gives up something considered less important by one so that one may gain something significant to fulfil one's goals. In this way, one may minimize one's losses, too, by not giving away too much, or giving away important elements.[51]

As Chu remarks:

In the business world, negotiators must always keep the

primary objective in sight and be willing to sacrifice the less important parts to preserve the more important elements of their agenda. This is the principle of giving the insignificant and in return gaining what is significant.[52]

12.   Claim the Wayward Sheep and Walk it Home

If the opponent offers an opportunity, capitalize on it and realize it to achieve one's purpose.[53] In a negotiation, it is possible for one's negotiating counterpart to act carelessly or unthinkingly sometimes and offer unsolicited concessions. One should immediately and decisively take them to one's advantage.

For instance, if you are negotiating to buy a brand new car and the salesman, eager and over-zealous, offers an attractive trade-in value for your old car, you should capitalize on this financial opportunity and enjoy a good bargain.

13.   Rustle the Grass to Disturb the Snake

'Snake' here symbolises either the hidden whereabouts of the opponent or the opponent's hidden intentions. In a negotiation, when one is unsure, one should be vigilant and watchful, observe and anticipate intently what one's negotiating counterpart is going to do. One should not take any action until one is, in some sense, certain.[54]

Also, if one is aware of the opponent's intention, one has an advantage with such knowledge. One should then pretend ignorance in order not to incur any suspicion, or prompt any unwarranted action on the part of the opponent.

It is only when one is ready and wants the opponent to reveal his or her intention that one then confronts the target and forces the discovery. When disturbed or forced, the revelation occurs. This will also catch the unsuspecting opponent by surprise.[55]

When this Strategy is used, it amounts almost to resorting to blackmail in certain circumstances. If you hold the trump card at the negotiating table, do not reveal it at an early stage. Instead, lead your opponents on. When the time is right, bluntly confront your opponents and force them to be truthful. Your winning is at the expense of their carelessness and unpreparedness.

14.   Return the Soul in a Borrowed Corpse

A dependent person tends to ask for assistance often. If one finds that one's negotiation partner is very dependent, one can exploit such dependence to one's advantage through exercising control over him or her. Therefore, in actual fact, one expands one's power by increasing one's sphere of influence in and through another person.[56]

If you frequently ask for advice or help from another, beware that the other person may be expoiting you to his or her advantage. Sometimes, you may be the conduit pipe in a design unknown to you. Your so-called helper may be your worst enemy in disguise. Learn to be sparing in your requests for assistance. Learn to be self-reliant whenever you can.

15.   Entice the Tiger to Leave the Mountain

The tiger symbolises a very strong opponent. The mountain refers to the home court advantage occupied by the opponent whereby he or she feels territorially safe and invincible.[57] Dealing with a stronger and more powerful opponent in his or her home ground puts one at a psychological disadvantage, and may further incur material disadvantages.[58]

Chu draws the following analogy as an illustration of this Strategy:

> When the CEO [Chief Executive Officer] of a large U.S. company visits Asia on a business venture, it is like the tiger leaving the mountain. He leaves behind his impressive office building, factories, and his luxury car, replacing them with a hotel room, a taxicab, and the handful of aides travelling with him. He is left struggling

with a foreign language and the customs of a foreign land.[59]

Therefore, the smart negotiators should strategically discuss items of importance with their more powerful opponents in neutral surroundings or one's home ground. They then gain a psychological advantage by depriving their opponents of their paraphernalia of power which may be perceived to exist in the opponents' own office environment.

In employing this Strategy, the fundamental point to note is the environmental setting. Smart negotiators gain an upper hand by dictating the place of meetings most conducive to them. If one's opponents, in addition to attending to the agenda, have to adjust to an unfamiliar - sometimes even uncomfortable - environment, they are immediately placed at some considerable disadvantage. One may have already won the negotiation without beginning it, by cleverly displacing the opponents from their comfort zone thereby disempowering them. The psychological disadvantage experienced by one's opponents at having to tackle unfamiliar logistics can work in such powerful ways.

16.   Let Go in Order to Capture

One has to realize the fact that a desperate opponent can also be a dangerous one.[60] He or she, under crisis, may become more formidable for he or she may think that there is nothing to lose by resorting to extreme tactics. Therefore, in a situation in which one has a complete upper hand, the wise thing to do is to allow an opening for the opponent to enable him or her to be able to retreat. Hope of a retreat dilutes his or her enthusiasm, spirit or valour.[61] This Strategy demonstrates the clever use of a soft or gentle approach to ensure ultimate victory.

The best consequence produced by this Strategy lies in effective people management. Allowing another to preserve his or her dignity in the face of utter failure incurs a gratitude so great that there is no need for headlong confrontation. He or she would just quietly recede, while fully acknowledging your power.

17.   Trade Brick For Jade

This is the Strategy of baiting. One baits with something of the same kind but not of the same value (metaphorically, trading brick for jade).[62]

This is an instance where one is exchanging with one's negotiating counterpart something of lesser value for something of greater value. It has to be done in such a convincing and undetectable manner that the opponent is completely unaware of the tactic.[63]

In negotiating sessions, for example, you could begin some peripheral talk about the issues at hand. It is likely that your opponents may unwittingly offer invaluable opinions on a current situation, which you can usefully act on. Your small talk ('brick'), has produced profitable opinions ('jade'). To be an artful negotiator, one has to have a good, if not thorough, understanding of the psychological condition of one's opponent in order to predict as to whether or not the opponent can be tempted by one's bait.

18.   Catch the Leader in Order to Win

In order to win in a negotiation, one must identify the most influential person or the decision-maker on the other side. If one manages to convince the leader of the other side, one has a good chance of succeeding.[64]

To be able to convince the opponent, one must know oneself and the opponent well.[65]

In a negotiation, it is essential for one to identify the chief decision-maker of the other side. Convincing the chief ensures one's victory. If one persuades the chief's negotiating team, victory is still superficial as the chief has the ultimate say. Negotiating in the People's Republic of China offers an excellent example of the importance of dealing with the prime decision-makers. Most often, foreigners tend to deal with departmental subordinates who have no power or authority to negotiate ventures. A lot of time, energy and effort goes to waste in such instances. Correct preparation in advance in identifying the true sources of the seat of power is, therefore, seen as an essential pre-requisite.

19.   *Remove Firewood From Under the Cooking Pot*

Faced with irreconcilable issues, direct confrontation is impossible to solve the impasse. One should instead attack the root, rather than the symptoms of the problem. By examining the root cause, one may devise a way out of the problem. Tackling a problem head on only causes it to worsen.[66]
As Chu states:

> In today's political and business negotiations, difficulties can often be traced to a single individual whose function seems to be continually to stir up unnecessary difficulties. Rather than dealing with the problem he creates, efforts should be made to remove or discredit this individual.[67]

Similarly, if one is faced with an obstinate and strong negotiating counterpart, confronting him or her directly may be useless. It is far better to be subtle and manipulate the situation skilfully to ensure success.

20.   *Catch Fish in Muddy Waters*

When the opponent is internally weak or chaotic, it represents the ideal time to strike. Where there is calm and order in the opponent, you should generate some disorder in the opponent in order to deprive him or her of sound judgement. When the opponent is in a confused state, he or she may give in to your demands, believing that you have always been entitled to them.[68]

By way of example, if someone ensures that two parties, say partners in a firm, are quarrelsome, the emotional strain may eventually lead to their partnership break-up. The instigator then makes his or her move and snaps up a bargain because they will want to sell their business, or dispose of their business assets to share in the proceeds. Their own sense of urgency in wanting to sell will cloud their judgement in correct valuation and pricing.

21.   *Golden Cricket Sheds its Shell*

A cricket sheds its shell at a particular stage, flies away and leaves its shell behind. An onlooker may mistake the empty shell for the cricket.[69]

This Strategy teaches disguise. To all outward appearances, one appears to be functioning normally. Secretly, however, one may have made other plans undetected by the opponent. One causes the opponent to think that there has been no progress made, or that there is a stalemate, when in fact one is on target elsewhere.[70]

At the negotiating table, for instance, if you cannot get your opponents to agree to something crucial to you, pretend to drop that agenda for the time being. In the meantime, work on the resolution of other matters. Your opponents will be caught unawares when you are ready to strike afresh.

22.   *Shut the Door and Catch the Culprit*

In this Strategy, it is recognised that sometimes one has to confront a problem directly; or otherwise, the problem may get out of control. Then, one is able to identify the root cause and seek to remove it altogether. However, one has to be fairly certain of the consequences when employing this Strategy, or it may turn out to be counter-productive.[71]

When you appear to be engaged in a protracted negotiation and the matter reaches a stalemate, lingering around much longer will diminish your resources in terms of time, effort and money. It may thus become necessary for you to have frank discussions with the other side, seek the causes behind the stumbling blocks, and take drastic action where required. This Strategy exposes the utility of making hard decisions in appropriate circumstances.

This tactic is the reverse of the Sixteenth Strategy of 'Let go in order to capture'. The Sixteenth Strategy uses an indirect method whereas the present Strategy uses a direct method of overcoming the opponent.[72]

23.   *Befriend Those Afar and Attack Those Nearby*

This Strategy focusses on territorial ambitions. An opponent may seek an opportune time to overcome nearby competitors while maintaining friendly relations with those at a distance. Friendship with the latter is superficial and in fact deceptive, with the aim of misleading them and catching them off guard. As the opponent succeeds in overcoming nearby competitors and expands his or her sphere of influence, he or she will systematically draw nearer to those initially distant ones and repeat the process.

This Strategy, therefore, refers to the fact that you should trust no one because you will never know when you will be betrayed, especially by a competitor who appears to be a friend but who has a history of dishonest conduct. Such a competitor has only one aim in mind, and that is to make you drop your guard and eventually weaken and give in to his or her demands.[73]

Chu warns: 'In the business world, when you see an ally betray his other allies, do not assume that your relationship is so special that he will not eventually betray you too'.[74]

24.   *Render Help and Engulf the Victim*

This is a Strategy used by a strong negotiator to defeat the weak easily. By offering to help the weak, one can extend one's power and influence over the weaker party. Additionally, if the weak party is in trouble and requests one's help, it makes the situation even more legitimate for one to help with the aim of overcoming the weaker party eventually.[75]

In life, there are many unscrupulous lenders who come readily to one's aid when one is financially hard pressed. Some such lenders may go to the extent of demanding that securities be transferred to their names as transferees, and not as mortgagees or chargees pending repayment. If these borrowers default, they immediately claim to be owners of the transferred securities. Vulnerable borrowers have to be very careful that they do not fall prey to these financial eagles who help themselves more than others.

25.   *Replace the Pillar With a Pole*

'Pillar' here symbolizes the opponent's support system, or alternatively, the opponent's main focus. If one uses a device in order to weaken his or her major support or to alter the opponent's focus, the opponent is likely to change the direction of his or her ways. One can then safely concentrate on achieving one's aim without the opponent being a hindrance.[76]

If your opponent is strong because he or she has a very able assistant, enticing the assistant away from the organization will force him or her to look for someone else, thereby weakening his or her position and ensuring your own victory.

This Strategy, when practised on an ally, is to control the ally and cause him or her to perform in accordance with one's wishes. In this way, too, one expands one's strength, power and influence.

26.   *Point a Finger At S'ung When Meaning Kwei*

This Strategy makes a clever use of dropping hints. In Chinese culture particularly, avoidance of direct confrontation is desirable. In the event that one wishes to criticise another (metaphorically, Kwei), the method to be used is to point a finger at someone else (metaphorically, S'ung), so that the listener can extract the message subtly meant for him or her. In this way, one does not become provocative and yet the message is transmitted.[77] Chu remarks: 'Asians are trained to understand these hints, but foreigners often do not. I was present once when a group of Chinese were trying to impart some subtle criticisms to an American diplomat. The American did not understand that he was actually the one being criticised.'[78]

Of course, the listener must listen carefully and realize the intention of the message in order for this Strategy to work. In doing business with the Chinese, the Westerner is advised to listen carefully for subtle codes. Otherwise, the whole venture may turn out to be very costly if one misses an important hint.[79]

If you are in a Sino-Western venture and are dissatisfied with the way your local Chinese partners conduct their business, confronting them directly will cause them to lose face and you will lose their trust and friendship. You could, however, resort to this Strategy and criticise some other person for the same failing. Your Chinese partners ought to get the hint and mend their ways.

27.   *Be Clever But Pretend to Be a Fool*

Arrogance may cause one's downfall. This is because an arrogant attitude may cause one to feel superior, over-confident and prejudiced. Arrogance may also result in errors of judgement in some situations. Ultimately, one may be misguided by one's lofty ways.[80]

It is far better, even when one is strong and in a superior position, to be conservative and pretend to be weak, subservient, and non-threatening.[81] One does not then incur the suspicion or watchful nature of the opponent. Victory will eventuate when the opponent is caught by surprise and by his or her own miscalculation.[82] As Chu observes: 'When one faces strong opposition, it is best not to take premature action that may lead to defeat. One should instead play the fool, posing no threat, arousing no suspicion.'[83]

The corporate world is a highly competitive one. By showing off your abilities in the hope of climbing up the corporate ladder quickly, you may produce the opposite result because your competitors, acting out of jealousy, could be formidable adversaries. It is wiser for you to appear non-threatening and act in a low key fashion in order to attain your objectives.

28.   Climb Upstairs and Then Remove the Ladder

This is an enticing or tempting Strategy. One deliberately reveals a weak spot and entices the opponent to come forward. Once the opponent approaches, one goes back to being normal. The former subsequently finds himself or herself exposed and open to attack.[84]

For example, you wish to buy an expensive article. Without revealing your interest to the seller, you could deliberately point to a fault in the article, such as the wrong colour, or wrong shape, or even some perceived irregularity. The seller will be put in a situation to defend himself or herself, and may lower the price to procure a sale, thinking there really is some fault with the item.

29.   Flowers Blossom on Treetops

Despite the fact that one is not strong or powerful enough, one should pretend to be otherwise and seek a magnificent display of power and strength. This will cause the opponent to think that one is very strong and invincible. As a result, it will keep one's opponent at a distance.[85]

In a negotiation, if you display a strong personality and persist with some key issues while neglecting others (which are your weak points), you may cause the other side to misread your true intentions and give in. To prevent this Strategy from being used on you, you should always remain alert to your opponents' 'empty-tank talk', and as far as possible, discover the true state of affairs. Emptiness lies behind rhetoric. Learn to read between the lines.

30.   The Guest Turns to Host

Normally, an invitee to an event is under the direction of the others. With the use of this Strategy, one cleverly manoeuvres the situation and manipulates the host in such a way that one gains control and takes charge of the event, without the host being aware of his or her loss of power or control.[86]

This Strategy is seen as highly manipulative. One uses subtle means without resorting to obvious tactics and yet manages to gain control.

For instance, you may be asked to attend a meeting at the other party's premises. But, by being able to set the agenda and control the proceedings of the meeting, and knowing when you should walk away if needs be, you would be taking charge of affairs at hand. The ability to take control at the negotiating table is an important exercise of power, and may denote that you have the upper hand. This will cause the other side to be wary, and cause confusion in his or her judgement.

31.   *Beauty Trap*

The exploitation of sexual desire for the purpose of achieving a successful negotiation has become classic. This is a Strategy of intrigue, subtlety and cunning. It also represents the use of external or outside agencies for the fulfilment of one's objectives.[87]

Strategically, every wily negotiator knows how to employ this means virtually at any stage of the negotiation. To cite Chu,

> Even in today's business world, the gift of women is not uncommon in Asian societies. It is the host's duty to understand tacitly and provide for the desires of the guests. It is felt that the barrier between host and guest, buyer and seller, may be removed in an atmosphere of wine, women, and song, and a close business relationship achieved.[88]

In the context of failing negotiations, this Strategy may have the effect of softening the opponent and eventually produce an agreement.

32.   Empty City Trap

When one is in a position of weakness, one should not let the opponent discover the true situation. Instead, one should continue pretending and carrying on as normally as possible, making the opponent believe that one is still at full strength. This will intimidate the opponent, causing him or her to be wary of one's perceived strength.[89]

This is a delaying Strategy. With time, one may recover one's resources and feel fresh again to tackle the problem. The 'empty city' refers to the lack of resources faced by one which, if discovered by the opponent, will lead one to doom. However, by cleverly concealing the true fact and creating the reverse impression, one is then able to buy time to recover one's strength once again.[90]

As an example, a company may not be doing well financially and it may even be public knowledge that cost cutting measures are underway. However, in order to continue to attract clientele, the company has to keep up with external appearances, like lavishly spending on advertisements, beautifying its reception area, or, if situated on landed property, improving its landscaping. The big picture continues to be exhibited to the public while the small picture is hidden away, thereby disguising the true state of affairs. People are, in general, taken in by appearances and impressions. They may then misjudge the situation and continue to feel confident about the viability of this company.

33.   Espionage

The tactic of spying is to obtain information relating to the opponent.[91] Information is power. At the negotiating table, the more one is armed with the knowledge of the opponent's condition, the more probable it is for one to win. By using the opponent's informants, one succeeds without expending one's efforts or resources.[92]

In modern times, industrial espionage is fairly common.

It is said that Japan's rise as an industrial power would not have been possible if not for its imitation and innovation of Western technology. Refining and fine-tuning is less costly than launching massive research and development in the invention of new technology.[93]

Westerners are often unwary of the Chinese inquisitiveness. They may dismiss it as pure curiosity when in fact, the Chinese are busy gathering information during a negotiation to enhance their own position. Questions posed which, at first glance, may seem innocent enough, could help gather information which leads the Chinese party to deduce certain important conclusions. For example, an answer like 'This is my first trip to an Asian country' could reveal the fact that this Western negotiator may be handicapped in personal experiences with Asians in general. He or she may have studied Asia, may have absorbed relevant intellectual knowledge, but may still lack the vital experience necessary in forging personal links which are crucial in relationship-building in Chinese businesses.

The other aspect of espionage is to plant false information deliberately in order to mislead the opponent and induce his or her misjudgement.[94]

34.   Bodily Torture

No one likes to inflict bodily injury on oneself. This Strategy demonstrates that one's genuine suffering of bodily harm will convince one's opponent of one's sincerity, loyalty and commitment, even though one is doing no more than feigning such traits. Physical suffering from self-inflicted wound is very persuasive and can often pull the wool over the opponent's eyes.[95]

This Strategy should be used almost as a last resort due to the fact that if this tactic is seen through by the opponent, one would have undergone needless bodily torture. There is pain, but no gain.[96]

Hunger strikes, a common ploy, are examples of the employment of this Strategy.

35.   Chain Links

Sometimes, one finds oneself unable to defeat the opponent through the application of a particular tactic. This Strategy is applied to help one win by exhausting the opponent through the employment of a succession of crafty techniques and artful means. Just like the links in a chain, one tries one method followed by another and continues the process with a multiplicity of tactics. The opponent will ultimately be defeated.[97]

This Strategy is not recommended if one hopes for instant success, since it involves a period of time and relies on a gradual depletion of the opponent's power or resources for success to eventuate.

36.   Running Away is the Best Strategy

A Chinese maxim says: 'Retreat is another form of advance. A good person does not fight a losing battle'.[98] Success and failure may be perceived as temporal matters. If one conserves oneself rather than annilate one's resources completely, there may be a time in the future when one can make a comeback. This is to reverse one's fortunes in due course.[99]

Escaping requires courage and boldness and a sense of good judgement, too. When one escapes as the situation so requires, one may live to fight yet another day.[100]

The process of negotiation may be viewed similarly. On reaching an impasse, hasty action may be hugely detrimental to one's interests; non-action may cause one to spend one's energy worrying and fretting and becoming anxious. During such times, walking away seems to be the best. It also provides one with a cooling-off period for one to re-consider the venture. Sometimes, it could even mean that other opportunities may surface and one is able to make use of these new opportunities.

Conclusion

Seen in the light of The Thirty-Six Strategies, negotiation is primarily a form of artful communication. One is often driven by one's desire to win, but winning is not always a matter of power and strength, or material wealth. Strategic negotiation enables negotiators to use their power of intellect, their understanding of the human psyche, and their sense of sound judgement to succeed where others may fail. While one's personal ethics may prevent one from engaging in certain strategies or tactics in a negotiation, it is important for an enlightened negotiator to be wary of the opponent's possible devious ways.

One can only hope for honesty, honour and fair play. But, more often than not, the reality is that our world is one of cunning, trickery and treachery. The Chinese are no less knowledgeable about the darker side of human nature than others, having had thousands of years of experience. The Thirty-six Strategies go some way towards helping them face up to adversarial situations.

Westerners who are uninformed of The Thirty-six Strategies may be profoundly at a disadvantage in Sino-Western negotiating situations. Deceptive and distracting tactics abound. The ability to recognise the use of any such strategy can help a negotiator prepare himself or herself for a formidable adversary.

NOTES

1   Geert Hofstede, *Cultures and Organizations: Intercultural Cooperation and Its Importance for Survival*, Harper Collins Publishers, London, 1994, at pages 171-172.

2   Geert Hofstede, note 1 above, at pages 171-172.

3   Geert Hofstede, note 1 above, at pages 171-172.

4   Chin-ning Chu, *The Asian Mind Game: Unlocking the Hidden Agenda of the Asian Business Culture - A Westerner's Survival Manual*, Rawson Associates, New York, 1991, at page 13.

5   Thomas Cleary (trans.), *Sun Tzu: The Art of War*, Shambhala, Boston & London, 1988, at page VII.

6   Chin-ning Chu, note 4 above, at page 196.

7   Chin-ning Chu, note 4 above, at pages 43-44.

8   I went to a Mandarin primary school in the Malaysian village of Paloh where I was taught classical Chinese culture and had to learn Chinese folk literature, phrases, idioms and proverbs amongst which were 'The Thirty-Six Strategies'.

9   Chin-ning Chu, note 4 above, at page 44.

10 Chin-ning Chu, note 4 above, at pages 75-76; Mandarin text - HO Sung Sin (ed.), *The Militaristic Thirty-Six Strategies*, Kwai Chey Private Limite, Hong Kong, at pages 168-173; Mandarin text - SIA So Zi and CHUI Kuo Chern (ed.), *Understanding Sun Tzu's Art of War*, The Economy Daily Publishers, Beijing, 1991.

11 Chin-ning Chu, note 4 above, at page 16.

12 Chin-ning Chu, note 4 above, at page 13.

13 Chin-ning Chu, note 4 above, at page 14; Thomas Cleary (trans. & ed.), note 5 above, at pages 10 and 28. As a matter of fact, in ancient China, the perfect gentleman was a person considered to be both culturally accomplished and martially prepared, i.e., he had to be simultaneously a scholar and a warrior. Zhuge Liang and Liu Ji are historically outstanding examples of the scholar-warrior.

14 Chin-ning Chu, note 4 above, at page 12.

15 In recent years, various symposia have been organised on Sun Tzu's principles and their application to corporate management in many countries attracting diverse occidental and oriental audiences. Such symposia were organized, for instance, in Beijing in October 1990 (Mandarin text: LI Fei and MA Hun, *Ways of Warfare and Enterprise Conflicts*, The People's Publishers, Kwangsi, 1991, Reprint 1992, at page i) and in Kuala Lumpur in July 1992 (reported in a Chinese newspaper in Malaysia called Sin Chew Jit Poh, 10 July 1992).

16 An old Chinese proverb. Quoted in Chin-ning Chu, note 4 above, at page 12.

17 Chin-ning Chu, note 4 above, at pages 14 and 43; Thomas Cleary (trans. & ed.), note 5 above, at page 3.

18 Chin-ning Chu, note 4 above, at page 43.

19 Fung Yu-Lan (edited by Derk Bodde), *A Short History of Chinese Philosophy*, MacMillan Company, 1948, at page 138; John M. Koller, *Oriental Philosophies*, Charles Scribner's Sons, New York, 1970, 1985 (second edition), at page 256.

20 HO Sung Sin (ed.), note 10 above, at page 1 of Summary.

21 HO Sung Sin (ed.), note 10 above, at page 1 of Summary; Thomas

Cleary (trans. & ed.), note 5 above, at pages 12-13.

22   Thomas Cleary (trans. & ed.), note 5 above, at page 71.

23   HO Sung Sin (ed.), note 10 above, at pages 1-2 of Summary.

24   Chin-ning Chu, note 4 above, at page 43.

25   Chin-ning Chu, note 4 above, at page 11.

26   Chin-ning Chu, note 4 above, at page 27.

27   Chin-ning Chu, note 4 above, at page 27.

28   Chin-ning Chu, note 4 above, at page 71.

29   The sources are mainly derived from HO Sung Sin (ed.), note 10 above; SIA So Zi and CHUI Kuo Chern (ed.), note 10 above, and Chin-ning Chu, note 4 above, at pages 44-76.

30   HO Sung Sin (ed.), note 10 above, at pages 2-3; SIA So Zi and CHUI Kuo Chern (ed.), note 10 above, at pages 94-95; Chin-ning Chu, note 4 above, at pages 44-45.

31   Chin-ning Chu, note 4 above, at page 44.

32   Chin-ning Chu, note 4 above, at page 45.

33   *The Art of War*, VII: 12; Samuel B. Griffith (trans.), *Sun Tzu: The Art of War*, Oxford University Press, London/Oxford/New York, 1963, 1971, at page 106; Thomas Cleary (trans. & ed.), note 5 above, at page 94; HO Sung Sin (ed.), note 10 above, at pages 7-10; SIA So Zi and CHUI Kuo Chern (ed.), note 10 above, at pages 95-96; Chin-ning Chu, note 4 above, at pages 45-46.

34   HO Sung Sin (ed.), note 10 above, at pages 11-16; SIA So Zi and CHUI Kuo Chern (ed.), note 10 above, at pages 96-98; Chin-ning Chu, note 4 above, at pages 46-48.

35   HO Sung Sin (ed.), note 10 above, at page 11.

36   *The Art of War*, VI: 1 & 2; Samuel B. Griffith (trans.), note 33 above, at page 96; Thomas Cleary (trans. & ed.), note 5 above, at pages 99-100 and pages 114-115.

37   HO Sung Sin (ed.), note 10 above, at pages 17-23; SIA So Zi and CHUI Kuo Chern (ed.), note 10 above, at pages 98-99; Chin-ning Chu, note 4 above, at pages 48-49.

38   Chin-ning Chu, note 4 above, at page 48.

39   HO Sung Sin (ed.), note 10 above, at pages 24-28; SIA So Zi and CHUI Kuo Chern (ed.), note 10 above, at page 99; Chin-ning Chu, note 4 above, at page 49.

40   HO Sung Sin (ed.), note 10 above, at pages 29-32; SIA So Zi and CHUI Kuo Chern (ed.), note 10 above, at pages 100-101; Chin-ning Chu, note 4 above, at pages 50-51; Mandarin text- ZI Yi Cheng et al, *Success Through Strategy*, Military Science Publishers,

Beijing, 1991, at pages 76-81.

41   HO Sung Sin (ed.), note 10 above, at page 30.

42   Chin-ning Chu, note 4 above, at page 51.

43   HO Sung Sin (ed.), note 10 above, at pages 34-36; SIA So Zi and CHUI Kuo Chern (ed.), note 10 above, at pages 102-103; Chin-ning Chu, note 4 above, at page 51.

44   HO Sung Sin (ed.), note 10 above, at pages 37-41; SIA So Zi and CHUI Kuo Chern (ed.), note 10 above, at pages 103-104; Chin-ning Chu, note 4 above, at page 52.

45   HO Sung Sin (ed.), note 10 above, at pages 42-45; SIA So Zi and CHUI Kuo Chern (ed.), note 10 above, at pages 104-105; Chin-ning Chu, note 4 above, at pages 52-54.

46   Chin-ning Chu, note 4 above, at page 52.

47   HO Sung Sin (ed.), note 10 above, at pages 43-44.

48   HO Sung Sin (ed.), note 10 above, at pages 46-51; SIA So Zi and CHUI Kuo Chern (ed.), note 10 above, at pages 106-107; Chin-ning Chu, note 4 above, at page 54.

49   Chin-ning Chu, note 4 above, at page 54.

50   Chin-ning Chu, note 4 above, at page 54.

51   HO Sung Sin (ed.), note 10 above, at pages 52-55; SIA So Zi and CHUI Kuo Chern (ed.), note 10 above, at pages 107-108; Chin-ning Chu, note 4 above, at pages 54-55.

52   Chin-ning Chu, note 4 above, at page 55.

53   HO Sung Sin (ed.), note 10 above, at pages 56-58; SIA So Zi and CHUI Kuo Chern (ed.), note 10 above, at pages 108-109; Chin-ning Chu, note 4 above, at pages 55-56; *The Art of War*, XI: 59; Samuel B. Griffith (trans.), note 33 above, at page 140.

54   HO Sung Sin (ed.), note 10 above, at pages 60-62; SIA So Zi and CHUI Kuo Chern (ed.), note 10 above, at pages 110-111; Chin-ning Chu, note 4 above, at pages 56-57.

55   Thomas Cleary (trans. & ed.), note 5 above, at pages 119-120.

56   HO Sung Sin (ed.), note 10 above, at pages 63-67; SIA So Zi and CHUI Kuo Chern (ed.), note 10 above, at pages 111-113; Chin-ning Chu, note 4 above, at page 57.

57   HO Sung Sin (ed.), note 10 above, at page 68.

58   HO Sung Sin (ed.), note 10 above, at pages 68-71; SIA So Zi and CHUI Kuo Chern (ed.), note 10 above, at pages 113-114; Chin-ning Chu, note 4 above, at page 58; Lucian Pye, *Chinese Negotiating Style: Commercial Approaches and Cultural Principles*, Quorum Books, New York et al, 1992, at pages 32-37.

59 Chin-ning Chu, note 4 above, at page 58.

60 'Do not press an enemy at bay': *The Art of War*, VII: 32; Samuel B. Griffith (trans.), note 33 above, at page 110.

61 HO Sung Sin (ed.), note 10 above, at pages 72-76; SIA So Zi and CHUI Kuo Chern (ed.), note 10 above, at pages 114-115; Chin-ning Chu, note 4 above, at pages 58-59; *The Art of War*, VII: 31; Samuel B. Griffith (trans.), note 33 above, at page 109; Thomas Cleary (trans. & ed.), note 5 above, at page 128.

62 HO Sung Sin (ed.), note 10 above, at pages 77-79; SIA So Zi and CHUI Kuo Chern (ed.), note 10 above, at pages 115-117; Chin-ning Chu, note 4 above, at pages 59-60.

63 Chin-ning Chu, note 4 above, at page 60.

64 HO Sung Sin (ed.), note 10 above, at pages 80-83; SIA So Zi and CHUI Kuo Chern (ed.), note 10 above, at pages 117-118; Chin-ning Chu, note 4 above, at pages 60-61.

65 *The Art of War*, III: 31 and X: 26.

66 HO Sung Sin (ed.), note 10 above, at pages 86-90; SIA So Zi and CHUI Kuo Chern (ed.), note 10 above, at pages 119-120; Chin-ning Chu, note 4 above, at pages 61-62.

67 Chin-ning Chu, note 4 above, at pages 61-62.

68 HO Sung Sin (ed.), note 10 above, at pages 91-94; SIA So Zi and CHUI Kuo Chern (ed.), note 10 above, at pages 120-122.

69 Chin-ning Chu, note 4 above, at page 62.

70 HO Sung Sin (ed.), note 10 above, at pages 95-99; SIA So Zi and CHUI Kuo Chern (ed.), note 10 above, at pages 122-123; Chin-ning Chu, note 4 above, at pages 62-63.

71 HO Sung Sin (ed.), note 10 above, at pages 100-104; SIA So Zi and CHUI Kuo Chern (ed.), note 10 above, at pages 123-124.

72 HO Sung Sin (ed.), note 10 above, at page 100.

73 HO Sung Sin (ed.), note 10 above, at pages 105-108; SIA So Zi and CHUI Kuo Chern (ed.), note 10 above, at pages 124-125; Chin-ning Chu, note 4 above, at page 66; ZI Yi Cheng et al, note 40 above, at pages 131-137.

74 Chin-ning Chu, note 4 above, at page 66.

75 HO Sung Sin (ed.), note 10 above, at pages 109-113; SIA So Zi and CHUI Kuo Chern (ed.), note 10 above, at pages 125-126.

76 HO Sung Sin (ed.), note 10 above, at pages 116-119; SIA So Zi and CHUI Kuo Chern (ed.), note 10 above, at page 127.

77 HO Sung Sin (ed.), note 10 above, at pages 120-123; SIA So Zi and CHUI Kuo Chern (ed.), note 10 above, at pages 127-128; Chin-ning

Chu, note 4 above, at page 67.

78   Chin-ning Chu, note 4 above, at page 67. At this juncture, it is useful to recall that the majority of Westerners are accustomed to low-context communication and hence, hint dropping on the Westerners may miss the point.

79   Chin-ning Chu, note 4 above, at page 67.

80   HO Sung Sin (ed.), note 10 above, at page 124,

81   *The Art of War*, I: 18; Samuel B. Griffith (trans.), note 33 above, at page 66.

82   HO Sung Sin (ed.), note 10 above, at pages 124-129; SIA So Zi and CHUI Kuo Chern (ed.), note 10 above, at pages 128-129; Chin-ning Chu, note 4 above, at pages 69-70; Thomas Cleary (trans. & ed.), note 5 above, at pages 88-90.

83   Chin-ning Chu, note 4 above, at page 69.

84   HO Sung Sin (ed.), note 10 above, at pages, 130-135; SIA So Zi and CHUI Kuo Chern (ed.), note 10 above, at pages 129-130.

85   HO Sung Sin (ed.), note 10 above, at pages 136-138; SIA So Zi and CHUI Kuo Chern (ed.), note 10 above, at pages 130-131; Thomas Cleary (trans. & ed.), note 5 above, at pages 90-91.

86   HO Sung Sin (ed.), note 10 above, at pages 139-142; SIA So Zi and CHUI Kuo Chern (ed.), note 10 above, at pages 131-132; Chin-ning Chu, note 4 above, at page 62.

87   HO Sung Sin (ed.), note 10 above, at pages 144-148; SIA So Zi and CHUI Kuo Chern (ed.), note 10 above, at pages 133-134; Chin-ning Chu, note 4 above, at page 71.

88   Chin-ning Chu, note 4 above, at page 71.

89   HO Sung Sin (ed.), note 10 above, at pages 149-152; SIA So Zi and CHUI Kuo Chern (ed.), note 10 above, at pages 134-135; Chin-ning Chu, note 4 above, at pages 71-72; ZI Yi Cheng et al, note 40 above, at pages 155-159.

90   Thomas Cleary (trans. & ed.), note 5 above, at pages 104-105.

91   *The Art of War*, XIII; Samuel B. Griffith (trans.), note 33 above, at pages 144-149; Thomas Cleary (trans. & ed.), note 5 above, at pages 77-78.

92   HO Sung Sin (ed.), note 10 above, at pages, 153-157; SIA So Zi and CHUI Kuo Chern (ed.), note 10 above, at pages 135-136; Chin-ning Chu, note 4 above, at pages 72-73.

93   Chin-ning Chu, note 4 above, at page 72. There is also a cultural aspect to the Japanese preference for innovation rather than invention. Japanese culture is also homocentric. Such a culture

constrains the daring and boldness of individual creativity, a necessary ingredient of inventions.

94   HO Sung Sin (ed.), note 10 above, at pages 153-154.

95   HO Sung Sin (ed.), note 10 above, at pages, 158-162; SIA So Zi and CHUI Kuo Chern (ed.), note 10 above, at pages 136-137; Chin-ning Chu, note 4 above, at pages 73-74.

96   HO Sung Sin (ed.), note 10 above, at page 158.

97   HO Sung Sin (ed.), note 10 above, at pages, 163-167; SIA So Zi and CHUI Kuo Chern (ed.), note 10 above, at pages 137-138; Chin-ning Chu, note 4 above, at pages 74-75.

98   Quoted in Chin-ning Chu, note 4 above, at page 75.

99   HO Sung Sin (ed.), note 10 above, at pages 168-172; SIA So Zi and CHUI Kuo Chern (ed.), note 10 above, at pages 138-139; Chin-ning Chu, note 4 above, at pages 75-76.

100   HO Sung Sin (ed.), note 10 above, at pages 169 and 171-172.

6 Case Studies In Sino-Western Negotiation

Introduction

The foregoing chapters have sought, in the main, to underline the divergent approaches to negotiation practised by the Chinese and the Westerners resulting in the relational style in the former and the transactional style in the latter. Mention, too, has been made of the fact that an ignorance of such a deep cultural dichotomy breeds misunderstanding and defeats effective communication.

In this chapter, six factual illustrations of Sino-Western negotiation will be used to analyse the potential pitfalls of unenlightened cross-cultural interaction as well as the factors contributing to successful Sino-Western negotiation. Additionally, in this chapter, I shall attempt to outline ways in which Sino-Western negotiation may be improved.

The case studies have been selected at random in order to provide practical value to the average cross-cultural negotiator. Selecting only cases which involve multi-million dollar deals may make the average person feel that my analysis is irrelevant to simple, everyday situations. This, however, is not true. When one makes cross-cultural blunders, one makes them whatever the circumstances. It is only that in multi-million dollar situations, the lessons are too expensive. The high-powered international negotiator must, as such, be more alert and careful.

If, in our ordinary everyday life, we can become more aware of, attentive to, and enlightened about another's culture, and habituate ourselves with cross-cultural knowlege, we can then be more culturally prepared to handle high-powered international negotiation.[1] Our cultivated habits will enable us to act more instinctively, spontaneously and sensitively in cross-cultural contexts.

The road to global human understanding is long and tedious, awesome and challenging, but its rewards are unmatchable and a lifelong treasure.[2] Effective and meaningful communication is the aim of human discourse. An awareness of various meanings which occur in the different cultures is fundamental to establishing cross-cultural understanding. Negotiation is an activity which may be seen and devised to promote such cross-cultural understanding. In particular, Sino-Western negotiation and understanding, more than ever before, represents an urgent agenda. The Pacific Destiny[3] has to be taken seriously.[4]

Case Studies

1. General Sino-Western Negotiating Styles, Aversion to Litigation, Attitude to Education

Facts   Mr Harold James, a retired Australian businessman now living on the Sunshine Coast, Queensland, had been doing business with the Chinese in Malaysia, Hong Kong, Indonesia, and Taiwan for over thirty years. The business chiefly involved the import of timber into Australia.

He reminisced about his cross-cultural business days and pointed out that he initially found it extremely difficult to do business with the Chinese because they were very interested in establishing friendship first rather than dealing in business, that the Chinese were very secretive about their bottom line, and that they were non-litigious. They were also very particular about the foreign tertiary education of their children, a characteristic which used to puzzle him but which, in later years, he saw with wisdom.

With regard to establishing friendships, he narrated that he and the other Australian businessmen, who first went to Malaysia to begin the business of timber export, found it very disorienting and unsettling to have to cope with the Chinese style of getting to know people first and building up trust before dealing in business. They virtually had to sit through many sumptous and lengthy dinners and were entertained night after night. On occasions, their Chinese hosts also supplied women companions. He was astonished by the enormous sums spent by the hosts on entertainment alone.

He said that the Chinese counterparts would begin to do business once there was friendship and trust. Even so, it was very hard to discover the bottom line of the Chinese. Even if he thought he had won on pricing, he was never sure if he was cut short elsewhere. That situation amuses him to this day.

He observed that his Chinese counterparts cared little for written contracts and were non-litigious when contracts were breached. As a timber exporter, Mr James had to place a shipment order for the timber months in advance and had to purchase the timber from the owners of the sawmill at a particular price. But, he often found that prices were arbitrarily increased by the timber loggers, and several times the timber was sold to other buyers at such increased prices. He suffered losses as a result. He urged his local Chinese counterpart to litigate but the latter would not. Once, when he applied enough pressure, legal action was taken. However, that worsened the situation. That was because the timber industry in Malaysia at that time was one operated by family businesses. It was run by a closely knit community of relatives in both logging and sawmilling operations. The commencement of legal proceedings against one of them was seen as against them all, and this incurred their collective wrath. In Mr James' words, 'the whole timber industry jammed up against my local partner'. They could not get timber supplies from anybody.

What fascinated and impressed him most of all was the earnest emphasis placed on their children's tertiary education by his Chinese business counterparts. He had to assist these parents in securing tertiary places mostly in Australia and had to be godfather to most of these young adults upon their arrival in Australia. The family care he provided has turned out to be a source of continuing friendship between him and his business associates till today. In fact, he has come to regard some of these Chinese families as his own families whom he can easily depend on at any given time.

Analysis   What initially took Mr James and his Australian partners by surprise was nothing more than a fundamental difference in culture and its shaping of the different negotiating styles of the Chinese and the Westerners. The Chinese, being a homocentric people, are accustomed to establishing friendships, developing relationships and building trust. People come before things.[5] Therefore, before they decide to deal in business, they must be able to regard their business counterparts as trusted friends who would go through thick and thin with them on a long term basis.[6] In their early associations with Mr James, they immediately displayed their relational style of negotiation whilst Mr James was expecting a transactional approach, - i.e., getting down to business speedily, an approach which, as a Westerner, he was familiar with.

In respect of the female companions, depending on the circumstances, the supply of these women could be seen as being a genuine gesture of warm hospitality. Alternatively, in the strategic sense, it could be interpreted as being the practice of The Thirty-First Strategy on Beauty Trap.

The bottom line with the Chinese is normally hard to discern. The suggestion of a bottom line itself implies a gain which may be quantifiable, measurable and obtainable in the short term. Hence, in the Western transactional approach which emphasizes dealings and short term benefits, the bottom line is perceived to be supremely important.[7]

By way of contrast, the Chinese relational approach places importance on relationships and long term objectives before short-term profits. Pricing is an essential factor, and while they expect to make a profit, the Chinese businessperson's perception and determination of pricing is also motivated and guided by other factors present in a business relationship. This is due to the interplay of a variety of factors in a business relationship considered to be relevant by the Chinese.[8] In this connection, it is also pertinent to note what Confucius said: 'If one is guided by profit in one's actions, one will incur much ill will'.[9]

The Westerners may tend to think that the Chinese are secretive about their bottom line, or that the Chinese may give a low price but regain the loss from elsewhere. Their frustration is, more often than not, a consequence of an inadequate cultural appreciation. In cases in which the Chinese have developed firm friendships with their Western counterparts, the Chinese bottom line is mutual gain. Such a conception of bottom line is diametrically opposite to the Western notion of bottom line which excludes mutuality. Also, where long term goals are contemplated rather than short term ones, it is culturally incongruous to imply any bottom line.[10] Of course, in certain instances where the foundation of friendship is not strong enough, or where the circumstances of the business dealing make profit-centredness the prime objective, the Chinese may resort to operating on a bottom line based on the Western notion.

The Chinese are generally not predisposed to written contracts and to litigation for alleged breaches of contractual terms. In Mr James' case, there was manipulation in the timber industry and his losses were the consequence of a certain amount of unfair play. Otherwise, the Chinese generally regard written contracts containing specific details as restricting flexibility. Their cultural inclination towards non-litigiousness is well-known. The Chinese prefer to resolve conflicts through informal means so that social harmony can be preserved. The outcome of litigation may enable a party to win the lawsuit, but the successful party may lose much more in other ways, especially social support and approval. Since it is not uncommon for families to operate related businesses together,[11] resort to litigation in the situation mentioned earlier had a wider implication: being a collectivistic people, the lawsuit against one was perceived and deemed to be against them all.

The emplacement of one's child in the care of another in furtherance of the child's tertiary education epitomizes Chinese culture microscopically. The Confucian insistence on moral virtues may be cultivated through scholarly learning. Education has thus come to be highly valued by the Chinese in general. It was therefore quite natural for Mr James' Chinese business counterparts to request him to help in securing Australian University placements for their children. Additionally, by entrusting their children in the care of their foreign business partner, they sought to bestow trust and respect necessary in any friendship, because of their instinctively relational ways. The provision of such family care is considered by the Chinese to be part of the equation in a business relationship, and they would be more than likely to behave more flexibly in their business dealings with their foreign partners as a consequence.[12]

The friendship arising from such trust also creates a dependency factor triggering off elements like *guan-xi* (personal relations), *ren-ch'ing* (personal goodwill), and *pao* (reciprocation), cultural factors which we have noted to be important and relevant in Chinese relationship-building. This explains, too, the fact that Mr James has happily continued with his lifelong friendships with the Chinese even though he is now retired from business. He warmly and genuinely refers to them as 'my brothers', and perpetuates his role as an uncle to their offspring.

2. Trustworthiness in Word

Facts   Two years ago, my husband and I decided to buy a new car. One of the automobile companies on the Gold Coast, Nissan, had a car sent to our home for a test-drive. We invited the car salesman, Tony, into the house, had tea and chatted. In the end, we told him that we liked the car very much but wanted to think it over. But Tony was very persuasive and persisted on a sale: in fact, he literally would not leave the house until we said we would purchase the car. Eventually, we agreed on a trade-in value for our existing car. Tony's superior said that the trade-in value, which was unusually high, was conditional on our same day purchase of the new Nissan.

Such a condition posed a problem to me. I have a habit of not committing to an acquisition until I know for certain that our financial resources permit it. Tony said it was usual to enter into a conditional contract and make a purchase subject to bank finance. In this way, Nissan would keep to the promised trade-in value and we could withdraw from the purchase if the bank finance fell through. The idea of a conditional contract did not appeal to me at all. I wanted to be certain that funds were available for the purchase. I told him that he could trust my word, and that once the bank finance came through, he was assured of a sale, on the basis of the Chinese way of doing things, that is, an oral promise would be honoured without it having to be in writing.

Tony was caught in a cross-cultural drift. But, to his credit, he became culturally sensitive to my proposition and agreed. Our bank finance approval came within the next couple of days and Tony secured the sale. He later admitted that he had learnt a valuable cross-cultural lesson to help him deal with Asians in the future.

Analysis   In this Sino-Western interaction, both parties exhibited respectively deep cultural traits. On Tony's part, he came to make a sale, adopted a transactional approach in his negotiating strategy, and insisted on a written contract to make both parties abide by their promises. On my part, I acted instinctively in making friends first before focussing on the car purchase, thereby manifesting a relational style in my negotiation, and having had trustworthiness inculcated in me, desisted from agreeing to a written contract.

I have been brought up to believe in this moral value of trust deeply, i.e., one should always honour one's word and keep to one's promise.[13] One has one's conscience to contend with, not any allegedly broken contractual promises to litigate in a court of law. Interestingly, I continue to uphold this personal belief despite my substantial Western education, and in spite of the fact that I am also a Contracts lawyer trained in the Common Law Justice System.[14] Although my own professional training inclines towards written contracts, given suitable opportunity, I would still prefer to behave and act culturally as a Chinese.

In this case, Tony was able to make a sale by his ability to perceive and receive a cultural insight, though he was disoriented by the strangeness. Even if his insight had been prompted by commercial expediency, the fact remains that he was made aware of the diversity of commercial approaches motivated by different cultural considerations.

It is relevant to note, too, that in every negotiation - whether intercultural or intracultural - the relative strengths of the parties will tilt the balance in favour of the more advantageous party. In this case, I possess both the Chinese and Western cultural insights but had chosen to act Chinese. My choice was facilitated by the fact that I had the power to buy any make of car, whereas Tony in this case had Hobson's choice: to make or break a sale. The commercial reality enabled Tony to learn a cross-cultural lesson which he otherwise would not or might not have had.

3. Chinese Cultural Negotiating Traits: Friendship & Trust, Bargaining & Face, Gathering Information, Personal Advertising

Facts   Mr Allan Manton is an Australian who used to work as a Building & Design Consultant with the former Dominion Homes on the Gold Coast, Queensland. His primary clientele were the Chinese from Singapore. He flew to Singapore regularly to hold marketing seminars and his business was brisk. His company had the foresight to put him in charge of the Asian market on account of his previous experiences in Asia. Several years ago, Mr Manton lived in Thailand and Hong Kong for a number of years and during those times, acculturated himself to some of the Asian habits and ways.

   When he first started selling homes in Singapore, he would, as far as possible, try to obtain Singaporean contacts from their friends and relatives resident in Australia. He would then communicate with these contacts from here and inform them of his proposed visit to Singapore. He built up such a good network through his existing clientele that on many occasions he experienced the beneficial snowballing effect from his network.

   He recalled one of his Singaporean clients whom he has since got to know quite well. At one of his initial marketing seminars in Singapore, this lady customer was persuaded by Mr Manton to purchase a house to be built in Burleigh Waters in Queensland. She then bargained with him for a discount and subsequently made out a deposit for a house. In due course, Mr Manton discovered that she had also taken a trip to the Gold Coast to check out the builder, the prevailing local property market, to make an investigation on Mr Manton and to ascertain that Mr Manton had sold her the house at the price that the local residents were buying at and not at any other inflated foreigner's price. Having been satisfied with her investigation, she proceeded to complete her purchase. With time, they developed a firm friendship and during the time that they got to know each other well, in less than a twelve-month period, she bought a few houses off Mr Manton. Additionally, she has encouraged many other relatives and friends to buy homes from Mr Manton.

Mr Manton said that he started to get many visits from Singaporeans who were interested customers and it was very important for him to take them out to 'yum cha' (to have Chinese snacks at restaurants). These occasions served to foster friendship and trust between the parties.

He was especially amazed by the word-of-mouth publicity he was getting from his Chinese clientele. He strongly attributed his business success with the Chinese to his ability to win their trust, and maintain ongoing relationships. He had learnt to adapt to the Chinese cultural behaviour of entertaining and being entertained at meals, and being interested in their welfare. He also realized that he had to suspend his transactional style when he dealt with the Chinese.

Analysis   This again illustrates the Chinese relational approach to any business negotiation. Mr Manton was able to grasp the cultural reality of the way his clientele functioned, and handled it sensitively, resulting in his own commercial advancement. In his business negotiations with the Chinese, he found it necessary to suspend his own culturally-habituated transactional approach. By understanding the Chinese requirement for friendship and trust before business, he sought to first win their friendship and earn their trust and to continue to maintain a warm relationship with his clientele. He also realized that the easy and less time-consuming way to win friendship and trust was through the referral system, i.e., contacts given by local residents who were associated with and known to his prospective customers overseas.

Bargaining is a preoccupation with the Chinese. Any one who has conducted business negotiation with the Chinese will at once notice their predisposition to indulge in bargaining, discounting, and 'mooching'.[15] It is certainly human nature to be pleased with a good bargain. For the Chinese, bargaining bears a cultural dimension to it.[16] I have referred to the Chinese obsession with the face concept. Being able to come away with a good bargain is testimony that one's negotiating counterpart has given face to one. Such face-giving is highly appreciated. One then tries in the future to remember to reciprocate. One of the ways of reciprocating, amongst others, is by recommending one's network of relatives and associates to one's negotiating counterpart. In such a way, though a discount may be a short-term loss, there is long term gain as one's business improves with more customers.[17]

The investigative actions of the lady customer do not come as as surprise to one used to Chinese culture. We have noted that the Chinese consider gathering information a highly valuable activity. Such investigation is also consonant with Sun Tzu's teachings, particularly his timeless quotation: 'Know your self and know the opponent, you will win at all times'.[18]

Promotion and marketing by word-of-mouth represents a generally common and acceptable way of advertising by the Chinese. Due to the Chinese culturally relational inclination, it comes as a natural consequence that a satisfied customer is the best advertiser amongst his or her relatives and friends. The latter will be inclined to go to the seller because his or her reputation for being trusted and trustworthy has been tested by a kin or an associate. One thus immediately overcomes the first cultural hurdle and is welcomed right away into the Chinese business fold. What one needs to do thence is to keep maintaining the friendships and continue to be trustworthy. A breach of trust is a serious matter. It can destroy overnight all the good and hard work one has built over a considerable period of time. After that, any effort to restore trust and confidence will be an extremely difficult task.[19]

An interesting feature to observe in a typically relational style of negotiating as portrayed by this case is that there seemed to be no real negotiation at all, at least in the way familiar to a culture accustomed to transactional behaviour. Because of the significance placed on relationships rather than the transactions themselves, the Chinese lady here felt, once Mr Manton was able to gain her trust and confidence, that she was able to let Mr Manton close deals for her. Such behaviour may seem baffling, and even dangerous or reckless, to a people used to transactional negotiation. This is because in a transactional culture, individual rights are sacrosanct, and parties' perspectives are more short-term driven. A relational culture tends to value people before things; it is not unusual or uncommon for a relational person to entrust another, with whom friendship, trust and harmony exists, with his or her possessions.

4. General Principles in Contracts

Facts Mr David Tan is a Chinese-Malaysian businessman. He owns a shipping business in Malaysia, dealing mainly with petroleum companies for the carriage of crude oil by sea. He has been in this business for over thirty years.

In his contract negotiation experiences with the Westerners, he has found them to be rigid, specific, and predisposed to details. The petroleum companies, which are multinational corporations, insist on using their standard form contracts which are detailed and precise. The Chinese, on the other hand, like to agree on general principles broadly defined. The Chinese prefer to cover all and sundry: in accordance with the maxim which goes 'cover the mountains and cover the seas' which means that one tries to include everything without being specific. Specificity may mean that one may omit something inadvertently. The Chinese tend to leave many items for subsequent interpretation. Their preference is for ambiguity so that there will be leeway in the future for either party to respond to changing conditions. He commented that such flexibility was possible because of the mutual trust that existed between the parties.[20]

Due to the basic difference in contractual approach between the Chinese and the Westerners, it is important to appreciate such flexibility and conduct business accordingly. He has relied on his cross-cultural experiences and knowledge to act in such a way which satisfies both parties.

Analysis   Mr Tan's Chinese persona and his personally accumulated cross-cultural experiences with the Westerners enable him both to accept Western culture and adhere to Western norms and to practise his own Chinese habits depending on the circumstances. In contract negotiations with his Western counterparts, his own cultural inclination towards general principles has to give way to the Western concept of incorporation of specific details in contracts. To cite Chu:

> Among themselves, Asians prefer a vague agreement because it leaves plenty of room for later adjustment if things aren't working out right. Asians understand that this deliberate vagueness is something that is neither understood nor accepted in Western business and in doing business with the West they have adapted the need for specific and detailed agreements.[21]

What Mr Tan abandons in ambiguity and flexibility in his instinctive style of negotiating contracts, he recovers in certainty and contingency. He accepts the fact that provisions have to be carefully made by both parties to minimize risks such that both parties are able to allocate commercial risks in advance and accept the likelihood of litigation in the event of breach.

5. Long Term Objectives

Facts   Mr Clarence Tan, a Chinese-Malaysian now resident on the Gold Coast in Australia, worked in the Money Market Division of Citibank in Malaysia until he resigned a few years ago. Before that he worked in Citibanks's office in New York. He said that Citibank, being an American corporation, emphasized Western-inspired qualities such as competitiveness and short term gains, particularly in the New York office. He lamented, too, that the American environment was such that each colleague looked after himself or herself and there was no real opportunity for forming firm relationships with anyone. The spirit of competitiveness dictated against any close relationship in the work place as each was viewed as a potential competitor or opponent.

Conversely, in the Kuala Lumpur office, Citibank had to respond to local realities and come to evaluate long-term objectives as important. In the money market, for instance, the Bank had to learn to absorb short-term losses in order to retain its existing clientele, especially the loyal customers of the Bank.

Interestingly, Citibank in Kuala Lumpur created a position for a Relationships Manager. This Manager was appointed to help cultivate and develop relationships with customers, with a view to personalising banking services. There is a strong suggestion here of a customer-driven management style.

Analysis Mr Tan's banking experiences within the same organisation but in two locations showed the two contrasting styles of Western and Asian business approaches. In the Kuala Lumpur office, had Citibank held rigidly to its Western philosophy of short term gains, it would not have been competitive enough in the Malaysian market. The majority of its Chinese clients would have transferred their businesses to other banks. It is important for the Chinese clients to detect the Bank's sense of 'reliability and continuity of purpose'[22] made possible by having long term objectives. The Bank's willingness to consider cross-cultural implications and to seek to modify its business strategy enabled it to subscribe to long term objectives and measure profits accordingly.

The provision of a Relationships Manager was an enlightened exercise. By being sensitive to the customers' cultural need for relationships before business, realizing the importance of maintaining such relationships, and by responding to this need creatively, the Bank was also able to capture a sizable market and maintain a powerful presence in the local banking scene.[23]

It needs to be pointed out the American environment is essentially an individualistic one, promoting competition and short-term benefits. Such a transactional style is inherent in the workplace as well as the market place. However, in the Malaysian environment which exhibits a collectivistic behaviour, the workplace may already be relational but the Bank had to introduce formally a relational style of business dealing by way of providing a Relationships Manager. This goes to show the Bank's recognition of the fact that a transactional approach is not workable in a relational environment. In short, the Bank's sensitive approach to its locale has helped to keep it a viable business concern there.

6. Cultural Taboo

Facts   Towards the end of 1993, a Gold Coast real estate agent, Ray White, installed a huge signboard in front of a house in the suburb of Robina for sale, with the words: 'DECEASED ESTATE' prominently displayed in large letters. Such a heading is very commonly used by real estate agents as a marketing ploy.[24] The implication is that prospective buyers might make a bargain purchase.

Analysis   Any prudent real estate agent would wish to cast his or her net far and wide to attract any potential purchaser, particularly in the face of stiff competition. However, linking a property with the notion of death serves only to make the Chinese shun it. This is because the Chinese are culturally averse to the idea of death or any of its associated suggestions. What is accepted in Western culture, in this case, is inimical to Chinese culture -- that is, death is taboo.

Ray White had difficulty trying to attract or convince any prospective Chinese buyer for an inspection with such a sale sign. This situation caused some concern as many current investors in South-eastern Queensland originate from Asian countries. Shortly after, they removed the original heading and replaced it with a more neutral one, but, needless to say, the damage had been done, and the Agency lost out on prospective Asian buyers. It is relevant to note that there were interested parties from Taiwan who bought two other properties on the same street[25] around the same time. Needless to say, these properties had not displayed signboards which carried taboo messages.

Improving Sino-Western Negotiation

Negotiation is a multi-faceted, multi-tiered, and multi-dimensional process. It is, therefore, virtually impossible to offer a comprehensive guide on how one should handle each stage of the negotiation process. This is made even more awesome in a cross-cultural context, as the potential for minsunderstanding and conflict lurks everywhere with each negotiator's own perception of reality and interpretation of behaviour based on his or her own instinctive frame of reference. I shall deal with six major and common points likely to occur in a Sino-Western negotiating situation in the hope that it will assist the Westerner caught in a cross-cultural bind.

1. Cultivating Cultural Awareness and Sensitivity

It cannot be stressed enough that it would do well for a Westerner intending to do business with the Chinese to familiarize himself or herself with some aspects of Chinese culture. The Chinese tend to appreciate any effort on the part of the Westerners to learn Chinese culture and customs. Such earnestness also goes to enhance relationship building. Cultivating cultural awareness and sensitivity will help to reduce misunderstanding, minimize frustration, and ease tension.

This requires, first of all, that the Westerner recognise that he or she is a product of his or her own culture. This represents an important first step. Such self-awareness is particularly relevant in a culture (the Westerner's) whereby one is usually so self-motivated or self-directed as to miss seeing that such individualism is itself a constituent of culture.[26] Westerners who tend towards such an individualistic outlook find it hard to grasp that they, as individuals, could generate a larger culture, as it were. Though they may accept that they are individualistic, they tend to dismiss the fact that collective individualism can produce any consistent or coherent behavioural patterns resulting in a culture of behaviour.   As such, the first step in an attempt at any cultural breakthrough is the realization or self-awareness that one is subject, most of the time unconsciously, to one's group culture.[27] In this way, one is more likely to recognise differences in another person's culture of behaviour, and more ready to invoke cultural empathy. Otherwise, the more likely outcome is an instinctive indulgence in ethnocentrism.[28]

2. Being Prepared

Thorough and unstinting preparation is absolutely essential when negotiating with the Chinese. This means that not only should the Western negotiators be sufficiently armed with the knowledge of their products or services, but they should also possess as much knowledge as possible about the backgrounds and connections of their Chinese negotiating counterparts. Bearing in mind the essentially relational nature of Chinese negotiation, the Westerners would do far better if they were to attempt acquiring people knowledge. For this to be achieved, preparation beyond knowing one's own products or services is a must.

3. Handling Ambiguity

To any Westerner accustomed to direct ways and frank means of dealing with people and things, it can often be an upsetting and frustrating experience having to cope with a culture steeped in indirectness and ambiguities. There is meaning and reason as to why the Chinese are fond of ambiguous behaviour, the primary motivator being the face-saving dictate. There is no need to feel exasperated. What might be more useful is an attempt at understanding the need of the Chinese party to engage in this necessary behaviour, and then trying to decipher the ambiguities.

Very often, one's intuition is the best guidance. If one is still unsure, and the subject matter is delicate but important enough, there are subtle ways of seeking clarification. The use of a trusted intermediary is one of the best ways.[29] The Chinese party would feel more at ease to disclose frankly to an intermediary who acts as a messenger, thus averting the possibility of losing face when dealing with each other in a personal and direct manner.

Where such an intermediary is not available, then, depending on the degree of relationship one has built with the Chinese party, it may be possible for one to seek direct answers, after acknowledging that one does not intend to offend.

4. Handling Contractual Attitudes

By far, the most difficult matter for the uninitiated Western negotiator to comprehend is the apparent lack of importance the Chinese attach to legally binding written contracts. Informal phrases such as 'Memorandum of Understanding' or 'Document of Intent' seem to preoccupy the Chinese more than firm contracts. At this juncture, it is helpful to recall the Chinese regard for personal trust and a desire to seal long-term ongoing transactions. Contracts are looked upon as demonstrating a lack of trust, temporary and expedient, that which can be breached or revised. Even if contracts are made, more often than not, the Chinese party tend to see these as documents to be filed away.

Such cultural attitude notwithstanding, most Chinese do understand the Westerners' desire for the printed word.[30] Cross-cultural, or rather, mutual, understanding of either party's cultural predisposition is an essential first step to resolving such a conflict. Once this understanding is achieved, whether or not one then presses on for a proper written contract rather than a mere memorandum of intent will depend on the degree of relationship one has managed to establish. The Chinese party who understands Western culture would appreciate that the Westerner's insistence on written contracts is not due to a lack of trust, but a habitual way of dealing and he or she would then become more at ease in such a situation. One, however, should be warned that even when contracts are entered into, there is an overwhelming desire on the part of the Chinese party for flexibility in interpretation and future implementation of the written contracts.[31]

5. Guarding Against Strategic Practices

Knowledge of the Thirty-Six Strategies is useful not only in one's opportune utilisation of them in appropriate circumstances, but more importantly, as the Chinese themselves often profess, in the timely prevention of these strategies on them.[32] The maxim 'Prevention is better than cure' cannot be seen as more relevant than in such Sino-Western encounters. One has to remain alert at all times and try to recognise any subtle strategic display.

6. Preventing Relationship Breakdowns

For a culture so accustomed to relationships, it cannot be reiterated enough that transactions are secondary to the success of the relationships between the parties concerned. As such, it is prudent to maintain the harmony and friendship achieved between the parties so as to enable a smooth ongoing business relationship. However, it cannot be ignored that inter-personal conflicts and friction are unavoidable at times. The golden rule to remember in such circumstances is to try to refrain from uttering unforgivable remarks: self-restraint in times of anger not only serves to preserve an otherwise already tense relationship, it also produces enduring benefits for the parties. This is because if angry remarks are exchanged in the heat of the moment which can cause the Chinese party to lose face, the friendship thus built may be lost forever which will, in turn, bear a negative impact on the business relationship. Such a behavioural rule contrasts sharply with typically Western behaviour whereby one is able to vent one's anger and afterwards to treat things as though nothing had ever happened and both parties again socialise normally.[33] In the Chinese context, there is no such thing as interpersonal open and fiery conflict and subsequent socializing.[34] A relationship that breaks down because of an aggressive confrontation may be irreparable. Hence, self-restraint is necessary. It is also a Confucian thing to do.

Conclusion

Hendon and Hendon remark:

> International business executives of the future are going
> to be challenged to take a more conscious effort to
> rediscover their own cultural programming and stretch
> the range of assumptions with which they have already
> been programmed. All the values, attitudes, knowledge
> and behaviour patterns in which they are cast must be set
> aside every so often to accommodate a different - perhaps
> even strange - combination of cultural assumptions of
> their foreign counterparts. The constant switching
> between cultures will have to be a swift and automatic
> thing. Insight, timing and flexibility are of the essence.[35]

The above illustrations have been given with the hope
that they provide useful insights into cross-cultural interaction
between the Chinese and the Westerners. Cross-cultural
knowledge, once understood and appreciated, may be developed
advantageously. It is only because of ignorance that there is
confusion, misunderstanding and frustration. When we are
educated as regards the differences and know how to react
appropriately, our sense of unease disappears. We become
enlightened; and we are more able to facilitate effective
communication.[36]

Sino-Western negotiation represents a fascinating and
seemingly complex field, one in which it is necessary to be cross-
culturally sympathetic in order not to be affected by any perceived
disorder or unsystematic behaviour. If we learn to discard our
own prejudices and become more open-minded, if we stop
looking for the familiar traits and learn to respond to the
unfamiliar and the unknown ways, we will improve not just our
negotiation skills but also our understanding of the intriguing
human psyche. In the process, we will have done humanity a
great service by closing gaps and fostering ties.[37]

NOTES

1   Donald W. Hendon and Rebecca Angeles Hendon, *World-Class Negotiating: Dealmaking in the Global Marketplace*, John Wiley & Sons, Inc., New York et al, 1990, at page 50.

2   Hari Bedi, *Understanding the Asian Manager: Working with the Movers of the Pacific Century*, Allen & Unwin, Sydney, 1991, at page 2.

3   The coinage is derived from Robert Elegant, *Pacific Destiny: Inside Asia Today*, Hamish Hamilton, London, 1990.

4   Robert Elegant, note 3 above, at page 12.

5   See John M. Koller, *Oriental Philosophies*, Charles Scribner's Sons, New York, 1970, 1985 (second edition), at page 246.

6   GOH Bee Chen, 'Understanding Chinese Negotiation' in (1993) *Australian Dispute Resolution Journal* 178, at page 180.

7   Edward T. Hall, *The Dance of Life: The Other Dimension of Time*, Anchor Press/Doubleday, New York et al, 1984, at page 105.

8   A trait similar to the Japanese: see Edward T. Hall, note 7 above, at page 105.

9   *The Analects*, IV: 12.

10   Edward T. Hall, note 7 above, at page 105.

11   See Gordon Redding and Gilbert Y.Y. Wong, 'The Psychology of Chinese Organizational Behaviour' in Michael Harris Bond (ed.), *The Psychology of the Chinese People*, Oxford University Press, Hong Kong/Oxford/New York, 1986, at page 280; John Kao, 'The Worldwide Web of Chinese Business' in (1993) 71 *Harvard Business Review* 24, at page 27; David Lague, 'Great Wave of China', The Weekend Australian, 12-13 March 1994.

12   See Chin-ning Chu, *The Asian Mind Game: Unlocking the Hidden Agenda of the Asian Business Culture - A Westerner's Survival Manual*, Rawson Associates, New York, 1991, at page 155.

13   David L. Hall and Roger T. Ames, *Thinking Through Confucius*, State University of New York Press, Albany, 1987, at pages 60-61; Chin-ning Chu, note 12 above, at page 244.

14   My undergraduate law training occurred at the University of Malaya in Malaysia, a country which has inherited the English Common Law Justice System. I was subsequently educated in the Universities of Oxford and Cambridge in the United Kingdom.

My doctoral studies were completed at Bond University in Australia, another country with a Common Law tradition.

15   Chin-ning Chu, note 12 above, at page 190; David K. Eiteman, 'American Executives' Perceptions of Negotiating Joint Ventures with the People's Republic of China: Lessons Learned' (1990) *Columbia Journal of World Business* 59, at page 62. See also Multicultural Times, 1 June 1994.

16   Chin-ning Chu, note 12 above, at pages 190-191.

17   For a parallel view with the Japanese, see Edward T. Hall, note 7 above, at page 106.

18   *The Art of War*, III: 31; X: 26.

19   Chin-ning Chu, note 12 above, at pages 243-244.

20   See Lucian Pye, *Chinese Negotiating Style: Commercial Approaches and Cultural Principles*, Quorum Books, New York et al, 1992, at pages 24 & 32.

21   Chin-ning Chu, note 12 above, at page 239.

22   Chin-ning Chu, note 12 above, at page 243.

23   Western culture has gradually come to realize the value of relational interaction. See Roger Fisher and Scott Brown, *Getting Together: Building Relationships As We Negotiate*, Penguin Books, New York, 1988.

24   For instance, see Gold Coaster, 25 June 1994.

25   Claremont Street, Robina, Gold Coast, Australia.

26   See William Gudykunst, *Bridging Differences: Effective Intergroup Communication*, Sage Publications, Newbury Park (California)/London/New Delhi, 1994 (Second Edition), at pages 42-43.

27   William Gudykunst, note 27 above, at pages 14 and 41.

28   William Gudykunst, note 27 above, at page 78.

29   William Gudykunst, note 27 above, at page 198; Chin-ning Chu, note 12 above, at page 248.

30   Chin-ning Chu, note 12 above, at page 239.

31   Chin-ning Chu, note 12 above, at page 239; Geoffrey Murray, *Doing Business in China: The Last Great Market*, Allen & Unwin, Sydney, 1994, at page 223.

32   Chin-ning Chu, note 12 above, at page 44.

33   William Gudykunst, note 26 above, at pages 197-198.

34   William Gudykunst, note 26 above, at pages 197-199.

35   Donald W. Hendon and Rebecca Angeles Hendon, note 1 above, at

pages 49-50.

36   See generally William Gudykunst, note 26 above; Geert Hofstede, *Cultures and Organizations: Intercultural Cooperation and Its Importance for Survival*, HarperCollins Publishers, London, 1994.

37   See Edward T. Hall, *The Silent Language*, Greenwood Press, Publishers, Westport (Connecticut), 1959.

Bibliography

Acuff, F. L. (1993), *How to Negotiate Anything with Anyone Anywhere Around the World*, American Management Association, New York.

Alford, W.P. (1995), *To Steal A Book is an Elegant Offense: Intellectual Property Law in Chinese Civilization*, Stanford University Press, Stanford.

Allinson, R.E. (ed) (1989), *Understanding the Chinese Mind*, Oxford University Press, Hong Kong/Oxford/New York.

Allott, P. (1990), *Eunomia: A New Order for a New World*, Oxford University Press, Oxford/New York.

Anderson, J.N.D. (ed) (1963), *Changing Law in Developing Countries*, George Allen & Unwin Ltd., London.

Astor, H. and Chinkin, C.M. (1992), *Dispute Resolution in Australia*, Butterworths, Sydney.

Bedi, H. (1991), *The Asian Manager: Working with the Movers of the Pacific Century*, Allen & Unwin, Sydney.

Barnlund, D.C. (1989), *Communicative Styles of Japanese and Americans*, Wadsworth, Belmont (California).

Berman, J.J. (ed) (1990), *Nebraska Symposium on Motivation 1989: Cross-Cultural Perspectives*, University of Nebraska Press, Lincoln and London.

Bo Yang (in Mandarin), *The Ugly Chinese*, Lin Pai Publishers, Taipei.

Bo Yang (trans & ed by D. J. Cohn and Jing Qing) (1992), *The Ugly Chinaman*, Allen & Unwin, Sydney.

Bodde, D. and Morris, C. (1967), *Law in Imperial China*, Harvard University Press, Cambridge, Massachusetts.

Bond, M. H. (ed) (1990), *The Psychology of the Chinese People*, Oxford University Press, Hong Kong/Oxford/New York.

Breth, R. and Kaiping, J. (1988), *A Business Guide to China*, Victoria College Press, Burwood.

Brady, J. P. (1982), *Justice And Politics in People's China: Legal or Continuing Revolution ?*, Academic Press, London.

Burkhardt, V.R. (1982), *Chinese Creeds and Customs*, South China Morning Post, Hong Kong.

Butler, A. (1994), *Tung Jen's Chinese Astrology*, Foulsham, London et al.

Capra, F. (1989), *Uncommon Wisdom: Conversations with Remarkable People*, Flamingo, London.

Casse, P. and Deol, S. (1985), *Managing Intercultural Negotiations*, Sietar International, Washington, D.C..

Cavusgil, S.T. and Ghauri, P.N. (1990), *Doing Business in the Developing Countries: Entry and Negotiation Strategies*, Routledge, London and New York.

Calero, H.H. and Oskam, B. (1988), *Negotiate For What You Want*, Thorsons Publishing Group, Wellingborough.

Chan, L.M.W. and Chen Bingfu (1989), *Sunzi on the Art of War and its General Application to Business*, Fudan University Press, Shanghai.

Chan, Wing-tsit (trans & comp) (1963), *A Source Book in Chinese Philosophy*, Princeton University Press, Princeton.

Chang, C. (1957), *The Development of Neo-Confucian Thought*, College And University Press, New Haven (Connecticut).

Chen, P.M. (1973), *Law and Justice: The Legal System in China 2400 B.C. to 1960 A.D.*, Dunellen Publishing Company, New York.

Chu, Chin-ning (1991), *The Asian Mind Game: Unlocking the Hidden Agenda of the Asian Business Culture --A Westerner's Survival Manual*, Rawson Associates, New York.

Chu, T'ung-tsu (1961), *Law and Society in Traditional China*, Mouton & Co., Paris/La Haye.

Cleary, T. (trans) (1988), *Sun Tzu: The Art of War*, Shambhala, Boston & London.

Cleary, T. (trans & ed) (1989), *Mastering the Art of War*, Shambhala, Boston & London.

Cleary, T. (trans) (1992), *The Book of Leadership & Strategy: Lessons from the Chinese Masters*, Shambhala, Boston & London.

Cleary, T. (trans) (1993), *Miyamoto Musashi: The Book of Five Rings*, Shambhala, Boston & London.

Cohen, H. (1980), *You can negotiate anything*, Lyle Stuart Inc., Secaucus (New Jersey).

Cohen, J.A. (1966), 'Chinese Mediation on the Eve of Modernization' *California Law Review*, vol.54, p1201.

Cohen, J.A. (1988), *Contract Laws of the People's Republic of China*, Longman , Hong Kong.

Cohen, P.A. and Goldman, M. (eds) (1990), *Ideas Across Cultures*, Harvard University Press, Cambridge, Massachusetts.

Conference Proceedings (1989), 'Negotiating and Arbitrating with Japan', Asia Pacific Law Institute, School of Law, Bond University, Australia, October 20-22.

Cotterell, A. (1988), *China: A Concise Cultural History*, John Murray, London.

Craig, J.A. (Reprint 1989), *Culture Shock: Singapore And Malaysia*, Times Book International, Singapore.

Creel, H.G. (1953), *Chinese Thought*, University of Chicago Press, Chicago.

Dalai Lama XIV (Tenzin Gyatso) (1990), *Freedom in Exile : The Autobiography of His Holiness The Dalai Lama of Tibet*, Hodder & Stoughton, London.

David, R. and Brierley, J.E.C. (1985), *Major Legal Systems in the World Today*, Stevens & Sons, London.

De Barry, W. T., Chan Wing-tsit and Watson, B. (compl) (1960), *Sources of Chinese Tradition - Volume 1*, Columbia University Press, New York.

De Bono, E. (1985), *Conflicts: A Better Way to Resolve Them*, Harrap, London.

De Bono, E. (1992), *Serious Creativity*, Harper Collins, London.

De Bono, E. (1993), *Water Logic*, Viking, London.

De Bono, E. (1993), *Parallel Thinking*, Viking, London.

Dennys, N.B. (1971), *The Folklore of China*, Tower Books, Detroit.

Dodd, C.H. (1982) (1987 2nd edition), *Dynamics of Intercultural Communication*, W C Brown Publishers, Dubuque (Iowa).

Doi, Takeo (1985), *The Anatomy of Self: The Individual Versus Society* Kodansha International, Tokyo & New York.

Edelman, J. and Crain, M.B. (1994), *The Tao of Negotiation: How To Resolve Conflict In All Areas of Your Life*, Judy Piatkus (Publishers), London.

Economy, P. (1991), *Negotiating To Win: A Manager's Handbook*, Scott Foresman Professional Books, Glenview (Illinois).

Eiteman, D.K. (1990), 'American Executives' Perceptions of Negotiating Joint Ventures with the People's Republic of China: Lessons Learned', *Columbia Journal of World Business* , p59.

Elegant, R. (1990), *Pacific Destiny: Inside Asia Today*, Hamish Hamilton, London.

Emerson, R.W. (1982), *Selected Essays*, Penguin Books, New York.

Faure, G.O. (1991), 'Negotiating in the Orient: Encounters in the Peshawar Bazaar, Pakistan', *Negotiation Journal* , p279.

Fisher, G. (1980), *International Negotiation: A Cross-Cultural Perspective*, Intercultural Press Inc., Yarmouth (Maine).

Fisher, R. and Brown, S. (1989), *Getting Together: Building Relationships As We Negotiate*, Penguin Books, New York.

Fisher, R. and Ury, W. with Bruce Patton (ed) (1981), *Getting to Yes:*

Negotiating Agreement Without Giving In, Penguin Books, New York.

Folsom, R.H. and Minan, J.H. (eds) (1989), *Law in the People's Republic of China: Commentary, Readings and Materials*, Martin Nijhoff, Dordrecht.

Folberg, J. and Taylor, A. (1988), *Mediation: A Comprehensive Guide to Resolving Conflicts Without Litigation*, Jossey-Bass Publishers, San Francisco.

Fung, Yu-Lan (edited by Derk Bodde) (1948), *A Short History of Chinese Philosophy*, MacMillan Company, New York.

Goh, Bee Chen (1982/83), 'Traditional Chinese Concept of Law, Justice and Dispute Settlement, with specific reference to the rural Chinese Malaysians', Unpublished Project Paper, University of Malaya, Kuala Lumpur.

Goh, Bee Chen (1993), 'Understanding Chinese Negotiation', *Australian Dispute Resolution Journal* , p178.

Griffith, S.B. (trans) (1963) (Reprint 1971), *Sun Tzu: The Art of War*, Oxford University Press, London/Oxford/New York.

Gulliver, P.H. (1979), *Disputes and Negotiation: A Cross-cultural Perspective*, Academic Press, San Diego.

Gudykunst, W.B. (1991) (1994 2nd edition), *Bridging Differences: Effective Intergroup Communication*, Sage Publications, Newbury Park (California).

Hall, D.L. and Ames, R.T. (1987), *Thinking Through Confucius*, State University of New York Press, Albany.

Hall, E.T. (1959), *The Silent Language*, Greenwood Press, Westport (Connecticut).

Hall, E.T. (1976) (Reprint 1981), *Beyond Culture*, Anchor Books/Doubleday, New York.

Hall, E.T. (1966) (Reprint 1990), *The Hidden Dimension*, Anchor Books/Doubleday, New York et al.

Hall, E.T. (1983), *The Dance of Life: The Other Dimension of Time*, Anchor Press/Doubleday, New York et al.

Hall, E.T. and Hall, M.R. (1987), *Hidden Differences: Doing Business with the Japanese*, Anchor Press/Doubleday, Garden City, New York.

Hall, E.T. and Hall, M.R. (1990), *Understanding Cultural Differences*, Intercultural Press, Inc.,Yarmouth (Maine).

Han, Suyin (1965), *The Crippled Tree (China: Autobiography, History, Book 1)*, Panther, London.

Han, Suyin (1966), *A Mortal Flower (China: Autobiography, History, Book 2)*, Panther, London.

Han, Suyin (1968) (Reprint 1988), *Birdless Summer (China: Autobiography, History, Book 3)*, Triad Grafton Books, London.

Han, Suyin (1988), *My House Has Two Doors (China: Autobiography, History, Book 4)*, Triad Grafton Books, London et al.

Hendon, D.W. and Hendon, R.A. (1990), *World-Class Negotiating: Dealmaking in the Global Marketplace*, John Wiley & Sons, New York.

Ho, Sung Sin (ed) (in Mandarin), *The Militaristic Thirty-Six Strategies*, Kwai Chey Private Limited, Hong Kong.

Hofstede, G. (1994), *Cultures and Organizations: Intercultural Cooperation and its Importance for Survival*, Harper Collins *Publishers*, London.

Hsu, Francis L. K. (1981 3rd edition), *Americans and Chinese: Passage to Differences*, The University Press of Hawaii, Honolulu.

Huang, Parker Po-fei, Chang, Richard I. Feng, Chao, Howard H., Hsia, Linda T. and Wang, Yen-chan (1967) (in Mandarin), *Twenty Lectures on Chinese Culture*, Yale University Press, New Haven and London.

Joy, R.O. (1989), 'Cultural and Procedural Differences that Influence Business Strategies and Operations in the People's Republic of China', *Advanced Management Journal*, vol. 54, p29.

Kao, John (1993), 'The Worldwide Web of Chinese Business', *Harvard Business Review*, vol.71, p24.

Kennedy, G. (1985) (Reprint 1986), *Negotiate Anywhere*, Hutchinson Business, London.

Kirkbride, P.S. and Tang, Sara F.Y. (1990), 'Negotiation: Lessons from Behind the Bamboo Curtain', *Journal of General Management*, vol.16, p.1.

Koller, J.M. (1970) (1985 2nd edition), *Oriental Philosophies*, Charles Scribner's Sons, New York.

Kremenyuk, V.A. (ed) (1991), *International Negotiation: Analysis, Approaches, Issues*, Jossey-Bass Publishers, San Francisco/ Oxford.

Kuhn, R.L. (1988), *Dealmaker: All the Negotiating Skills and Secrets You Need*, John Wiley & Sons, New York.

Latourette, K.S. (1964), *The Chinese, Their History And Culture*, MacMillan Co., New York.

Lau, D.C. (trans) (1979), *Confucius: The Analects (Lun Yu)*, Penguin Books, London.

Lee, E. (1985), *Commercial Disputes Settlement In China*, Lloyd's of London Press Ltd., London et al.

Lee Song Woo (1989) (Reprint 1990) (in Mandarin), *Thick Black Theory*,

Chiu Zee Publishers, Beijing.

Li Fei and Ma, Hun (1991) (Reprint 1992) (in Mandarin), *Ways of Warfare and Enterprise Conflicts*, The People's Publishers, Kwangsi.

Low, C. C. & Asociates (ed & trans) (1993), *Sun Zi's Art of War*, Canfonian Pte Ltd, Singapore.

Lloyd, D. (1977), *The Idea of Law*, Penguin Books, Harmondsworth.

Lubman, S. (1967), 'Mao and Mediation: Politics and Dispute Resolution in Communist China', *California Law Review* , Vol.55, p.1296.

MacKenzie, D.A. (1986) (Reprint 1992), *China and Japan*, Bracken Books, London.

Macleod, R. (1988), *China, Inc.: How to Do Business with the Chinese*, Bantam Books, Toronto/New York.

March, R.M. (1990), *The Japanese Negotiator: Subtlety and Strategy Beyond Western Logic*, Kodansha International, Tokyo & New York.

Mason, C. (1989), *Simple Etiquette in China*, Paul Norbury Publications, Folkestone.

McCreary, D.R. (1986), *Japanese-U.S. Business Negotiations: A Cross-cultural Study*, Praeger, New York.

McNeill, W. and Sedlar, J. (eds) (1960), *Classical China*, Oxford University Press, New York.

Mohamed Ariff (ed) (1991), *The Pacific Economy: Growth and External Stability*, Allen & Unwin, Sydney.

Moran, R.T. and Stripp, W.G. (1991), *Dynamics of Successful International Business Negotiations*, Gulf Publishing Company, Houston.

Moser, M.J. (1987 2nd edition), *Foreign Trade, Investment and the Law in the People's Republic of China*, Oxford University Press, New York.

Mulholland, J. (1991), *The Language of Negotiation*, Routledge, London and New York.

Murray, G. (1994), *Doing Business in China: The Last Great Market*, Allen & Unwin, Sydney.

Nakamura, Hajime (Revised English Translation Edited by Philip P. Weiner) (1971), *Ways of Thinking of Eastern Peoples: India, China, Tibet, Japan*, University of Hawaii Press, Honolulu.

Nierenberg, G.I. (1986), *The Complete Negotiator*, Nierenberg & Zeif Publishers, New York.

Nyce, R. (edited by Shirle Gordon) (1973), *Chinese New Villages in Malaya: A Community Study*, Malaysian Sociological Institute, Singapore.

Pan, Lynn (1990), *Sons of the Yellow Emperor: The Story of the Overseas Chinese*, Mandarin Paperback, London.

Pan, Yigang and Vanhonacker, W.R. (1992), 'Chinese and American Cultures: Value Structure and Family Orientation - An Explorative Study', Euro-Asia Centre Research Series, INSEAD Euro-Asia Centre, Fontainebleau.

Pryles, M. and Iwasaki, Kazuo (1983), *Dispute Resolution in Australia-Japan Transactions*, Law Book Company Limited, Sydney.

Pua Tao Fei (ed) (in Mandarin), *Sun Tzu's Artful Strategies*, Kwai Chey Private Limited, Hong Kong.

Pye, Lucian W. (1982), *Chinese Commercial Negotiating Style*, Oelgeschlager, Gunn & Hain, Cambridge, Massachusetts.

Pye, Lucian W. (1992), *Chinese Negotiating Style: Commercial Approaches and Cultural Principles*, Quorum Books, New York.

Richards, C. and Walsh, F. (1990), *Negotiating*, Australian Government Publishing Service, Canberra.

Roberts, S. (1979), *Order and Dispute: An Introduction to Legal Anthropology*, Penguin Books, Harmondsworth.

Rojot, J. (1991), *Negotiation: From Theory to Practice*, MacMillan, Hong Kong.

Rose, C. (1989), *Negotiate And Win*, SPA Books, Stevenage.

Rossbach, S. (1984), *Feng Shui*, Century, London.

Rubin, J.Z. and Sander, F.E.A. (1991), 'Culture, Negotiation, and the Eye of the Beholder', *Negotiation Journal*, p. 249.

Sinclair, K. and Wong, Po-yee Iris (Reprint 1993), *Culture Shock ! - China*, Graphic Arts Center Publishing Company, Portland, Oregon.

Schwartz, B.I. (1985), *The World of Thought in Ancient China*, Belknap Press of Harvard University Press, Cambridge, Massachusetts.

Scott, B. (Reprint 1989), *The Skills of Negotiating*, Gower, Aldershot.

Scott, P. A. (ed) (1978), *Man and Nature in Southeast Asia*, School of Oriental and African Studies, University of London, London.

Sia So Zi and Chui Kuo Chern (eds) (1991) (in Mandarin), *Understanding Sun Tzu's Art of War*, The Economy Daily Publishers, Beijing.

Smith, C.J. (1991), *CHINA: People And Places in the Land of One Billion*, Westview Press, San Francisco & Oxford.

Sogyal Rinpoche (1992) (Reprint 1994), *The Tibetan Book of Living and Dying*, Random House, London.

Stewart, E.C. (1972), *American Cultural Patterns: A Cross-Cultural Perspective*, Intercultural Press Inc., Yarmouth, Maine.

Stone, R. (1988), 'The Chinese Negotiating Game', *The Practising Manager (Australia)*, vol.9, p.27.

Stromholm, S. (1985), *A Short History of Legal Thinking in the West*, Norstedts, Stockholm.

Tay, Alice E-S and Leung, Conita S C (eds) (1995), *Greater China: Law, Society And Trade*, Law Book Company, Sydney.

Tung, Rosalie L. (1984), *Business Negotiations with the Japanese*, Lexington Books, Lexington, Mass./Toronto.

Tsunoda, Ryusaku, de Barry, W. T. and Keene, D. (Compl.) (1971), *Sources of Japanese Tradition*, Columbia University Press, New York.

Tu, Wei-Ming (1989), *Centrality and Commonality: An essay on Confucian Religiousness*, State of New York University Press, Albany.

Van der Sprenkel, S. (1972), *Legal Institutions in Manchu China: A Sociological Analysis*, University of London The Athlone Press, London.

Vaughan, J.D. (1977), *The Manners and Customs of the Chinese of the Straits Settlements*, Oxford University Press, Kuala Lumpur.

Walters, R.J. (1991), "'Now that I ate the Sushi, Do we have a Deal ?' - The Lawyer as Negotiator in Japanese-U.S. Business Transactions", *Northwestern Journal of International Law & Business* , vol.12, p.335.

Wang, Gungwu (1992), *Community and Nation: China, Southeast Asia and Australia*, Allen & Unwin, Sydney.

Weber, R. (1986) (Reprint 1987), *Dialogues with Scientists and Sages: The Search for Unity*, Routledge & Kegan Paul, London & New York.

Weiss, J. (1989), *The Asian Century: The Economic Ascent of the Pacific Rim - and What it Means for the West*, Facts on File, New York/Oxford.

Wilhelm, A.D., Jr (1994), *The Chinese At The Negotiating Table*, National Defense University Press, Washington, DC.

Wilhelm, R. (1979), *Lectures on the I Ching : Constancy and Change*, Princeton University Press, Princeton.

Wong, Cheng Tong (in Mandarin), *Sun Tzu's Art of War*, Zi Yang Publishers, Taipei.

Wong, Choon San (1967), *A Cycle of Chinese Festivities*, Malaysia Publishing House Ltd., Singapore.

Zartman, I. W. and Berman, M.R. (1982), *The Practical Negotiator*, Yale University Press, New Haven and London.

Zi, Yi Cheng et al (1991) (in Mandarin), *Success Through Strategy*, Military Science Publishers, Beijing.

Zimmerman, M.A. (1988), *Dealing with the Japanese*, Unwin Paperbacks, London, Sydney.

Index

ambiguity 30, 108-109, 176, 180-181
ancestral worship 52, 61, 65, 67
Anglo-Saxon 3, 23

body language 15, 110

Classical Age 48
collectivism 22-27, 88, 105
  ingroup 24
  outgroup 24
compromise 70, 86, 104-105
Confucianism 26, 48-54, 57, 63, 88, 117
  benevolence 52-53
  filial piety (*hsiao*) 52-53, 65, 67
  five cardinal relationships 26, 51-52, 87
  righteousness (*yi*) 52-54
Confucius 49, 52-53, 69, 168
contracts 7, 106-107, 113, 167, 169-171, 175-176, 181
cultural traits 89-111
culture
  role of, 17-19
  and language 20-22
customs 48, 60-69
  birth 62-63
  ching-ming 66-67
  dumpling festival 67
  funerals 64-65
  hungry ghosts festival 68
  marriage 63-64
  mooncake festival 68-69
  new year festival 65-66
  winter festival 69

delay in decision-making 103-104

egocentric 20, 23, 91, 118
egocentrism 27-29, 88

face 93, 95-99, 101, 109, 152, 174, 181-182
feng shui 111-114, 118
flexibility 105-107
frame of reference 5, 20, 179
friendship 91-95

gathering information 102-103, 156, 172-175
good memory 107-108
guan-xi 94, 98-100, 170

Han Fei Tzu 58
harmony 24, 26-27, 49-51, 53-54, 59, 69-70, 72, 86-87, 95, 97, 104, 111, 113-114, 118, 134, 175, 182
high-context communication 29-32
homocentric 20, 22, 27, 32, 38, 47-48, 62, 72, 91, 168
homocentrism 24-27, 38, 85, 88, 105, 118

individualism 23, 25, 27-29, 47, 88, 105, 179
Information Age 1, 5, 30

Japanese 6-7, 21-22, 26, 35, 87-88,
    102, 106-107
Judeo-Christian 49

Lao-Tzu 54, 57
lawyering skill 4-7
Legalism 48, 58-60
li 27, 50-52, 65, 86
lien 94, 96
long-term 33-34, 87-88, 90, 95, 98,
    100, 104, 106, 118, 168-169,
    174, 176-178
low-context communication 29-31

Mencius 62
mien-tze 94, 96
Mo Tzu 57-58
Mohism 48, 57-58

non-verbal communication 110-
    111

Pacific Century 1, 7-10
Pacific Destiny 166
pao 27, 75, 100, 170
patience 33, 88, 100-102, 118, 143
perceptions of law, justice and
    dispute settlement, 48,
    69-73
philosophies, 48-60
prejudice 6, 16-17, 36, 183

reciprocity 27, 87, 100, 105
relational 3, 27, 33-34, 38, 48, 54,
    58, 69, 87-88, 102, 118, 134,
    165, 170-171, 173-175, 177,
    180
ren-ch'ing 94, 99-100, 170

Sino-Western
    communication 10
    cultures 22-24
    interaction 7-8, 10, 171
    negotiation 6-7, 32-37, 117, 137,
        158, 165-183
    venture 152
status 108
Sun Tzu 88, 102, 105, 117, 133-135,
    174

taboos 114-117, 178
    colours 116
    numerology 114-116
    symbolism in gifts 116-117
Taoism 48-49, 54-57
    rang 55-56
    reversal principle 55-56
    wu-wei 55-56
task versus time concept 110
telepathy 15
Thirty-six Strategies 133-158
transactional 3, 33-35, 88, 118, 165-
    166, 168, 171, 173-175, 177-
    178
trust 7, 89-92, 95, 98, 106-107, 118,
    134, 143, 150, 167-168, 170-
    175, 181
trustworthiness 89-91, 170-172

yin and *yang* 135-136, 138